THE HEART KNOWS WHAT THE
MIND CANNOT SEE.

ISBN 978-1-9196204-0-4

This book is to be used for entertainment purposes only, and is not to be construed as medical, legal or professional advice. The author bears no responsibility for decisions made based on the advice contained within the book.

CONTENTS

FORWARD

This is a thought-provoking and enlightening exploration of spirituality and perception. The text functions as a guide to self-improvement, with a mixture of autobiographical elements and snippets of universal wisdom. The speaker provides accessible solutions to life's difficulties, and an outlook of optimism applicable to any circumstance. The illustrations and graphics are thoughtfully chosen, and the interactive textual elements give this work an originality that sets it apart. The speaker's own experiences and conclusions are at the heart of this fiction, and the first person narrative voice creates a sense of proximity between author and reader. The text describes itself as 'a journey to the heart', and this truthful discovery of the self is reflected in the speaker's revelation of his whole self through the text. The narrative often presents a dichotomy between positive and negative outlooks or voices.

For example, the speaker includes sections in which his self-doubt speaks, 'you've got no proper education, you can't spell properly, you're dyslexic and your grammar is crap. You're not really a writer'. This negative voice directly opposes the sense of self-belief the speaker builds within the narrative. He uses examples such as this to remind readers that the journey to happiness is complex and that flaws or setbacks are natural. The negative separation or fragmentation of the self is prevalent in the lines, 'I do not love the grumpy me, the sad me, the hostile me, the parts of me that act as if I do not care'.

The act of writing represents a unification of the self and an attempt to reframe the speaker's life into coherence. The frequent use of direct address and rhetorical questions promotes an active reading experience, in which the author opens up a dialogue with the reader. The text includes prompts and activities for the reader to engage with and learn from. Encouraging readers to take part in the text is emblematic of their journey to self-fulfilment and love, in which they must take responsibility for actively creating their own happiness.

The speaker depicts his process of enlightenment as a framework for others to emulate, and the format of the text demonstrates the transfer of agency to those who take part in the speaker's challenges at the end of each chapter. This work ultimately teaches us that 'we are the cause of what is' and thus sheds light on the crucial idea that every individual has the power to create themselves and their world positively.

INTRODUCTION

This book has no answers for you. It will always be, and must be, that you decide what will and what will not be. But it is my dearest wish that this book's story may mirror aspects of your own journey and so, shed light on the places in you where answers can be found.

In the journey described in these pages, I describe the truths I have found within myself. They were new to me, but of course, no different to the truths that have been spoken of for thousands of years, as the truth does not change. Although each epoch will describe the truth in the language of its time in its attempt to share the feeling of their meanings.

The books' purpose is to represent these truths in a style so that they can easily be recognised, yet still give space for more in-depth thoughts to be considered. It is a journey to the heart, about learning to love oneself and searching for the divine nature of being human. It delves into the workings of the mind, its power and why we do what we do. It uncovers the power within our vulnerability, and explores the creativity of the heart. It is an investigation and celebration of the meaning of being human. The writing is philosophical and, at times, poetic in an effort to express the ineffable nature of the deeper aspects of the heart.

While this book is intended to be a direct conversation with you, the reader, the journey to the heart requires from us a shifting of perspectives, so that we may attain a well-rounded understanding of the heart. You will encounter passages in italics that seek to enrich this journey by offering personal reflections of my own and differing perspectives for you to consider.

Throughout this book I have also included a collection of phrases that bring together the essence of what I hope to communicate to you. But like the rest of this book, they are to be taken or left as you see fit.

At the end of each chapter there will be ideas for participation and practices that I have used in my journey or have been created to help bring grounding to the chapter.

In this journey to the heart of myself, it became apparent that there was, within the heart, something far greater than I thought possible, something that was powerful and most benevolent. It may have been the soul, spirit, the higher self, source, universe, or God. I did not care what name it had. It existed and I wanted it – wanted to join this part of myself.

I was not brought up in any religion and was never really a God type of person. The word 'God' always seemed too 'out there', too separate from the deeply personal human journey. But as I got deeper into the journey to the heart, the need to describe this sense of greatness I found within me, became necessary. The word Source seemed, for me, too dry and academic and the word Universe just seemed too big and impersonal.

So, for the sake of brevity, the term 'God' has occasionally been used when referring to this something that is deep, big and powerful that I felt within the heart. The word feels singular and gives me the sense that everything is connected. It implies a person, which makes it personal. This seems fitting as life seems so very personal, full of intimate experiences that only we can know, only we can choose their meaning.

But I'm really not that bothered, it is in the end, just a label that I hang upon the great mystery of what I do not understand.

THE HEART KNOWS WHAT THE MIND CANNOT SEE

It has been said that the greatest regret of the dying is that they wished they'd been truer to themselves.

As if there is a life's purpose in being who we are.

As if who we are is a purpose.

As if within ourselves exists the flame of our happiness.

I don't want to look back on my life with regret, to feel that I have let myself down. Forsaken myself by misadventures at the behest of other people's shadows or the propaganda of the day. We cannot live another's path. Life is an intimate personal journey that only we can tread and a path that only we can see.

But where, within ourselves, do we go to find this truth of us, this thing of who we are that makes life worth living? Where is the source of our authenticity and what would truly make us happy? For they are intricately linked. We can never be happy without living the truth of ourselves.

This is my quest and so, the story begins…

I had always been driven by a passion for the truth; the truth of myself, and the truth of life. To know why we do what we do and to understand the forces

that cause what is, to be.

From the angsty teenager, searching for the meaning of life, to the somewhat chilled-out older man I now am. There has been a hunger that has never left me. It has been a great journey but life always has its moments. A few years ago, I found myself feeling desperate, depressed, and downright pissed off.

Despite years of spiritual endeavour, my life still seemed to be easily chaotic and its beauty fleeting. Any resemblance of lucidity dissolving all too quickly into the mundane or ludicrous.

Yet the years had taught me that life was no accident. Everything had a cause, a reason why it was so. A certainty that made what was and created what will be. This certainty was evident in the natural world; its reliability is used to calculate the heavens above and the activity of the tiniest molecule of life. But being human seemed such a different story. An experience that all too often seemed to have little rhyme or reason, leaving me feeling bewildered by wayward emotions and the wanderings of the mind.

My wish for any lasting freedom to my deeper feelings of life still eluded me. After all these years some piece of the puzzle of being me was still missing.

I felt let down by life, but worst of all I felt I had let myself down, dishonoured the happy, clear-eyed strident youth that I was. This me of me that had held such wonderful dreams of life, but I could not give up. This search for meaning was my life's journey, yet I had tried everything and now felt exhausted and hopeless.

There is no 'answer' out there because it is all a reflection of what we hold life to be.

When I had used up all the possibilities of something 'out there' to save me, to give solace and calm the turbulent waters of my heart, there was no other way to go, but within.

I sat at the kitchen table with myself. It was covered with the scribbled ramblings of years of search and thought. Writings that now seemed irrelevant in the face of what I was feeling. I stared out of the window into nothingness. Yet I wanted an answer, a real answer. Not a clever intellectualism or a vague feeling, I had enough of them.

I surrendered to the calamity of myself, letting go of all actions to ease the situation. I allowed myself to feel the catastrophe I was in...and waited for what I did not know, but I had nowhere else to turn. There was no action I could do, no thought I could think to help myself. I had nothing left but a wish for an answer to a question I did not know.

So, I drove inwards into the very core of myself, to a place I had never been before, nor even knew really existed. I embraced the whole of me, without conditions or expectations. Because I had nothing left to give, nothing to clothe my naked vulnerable self. I surrendered to an unknown me.

I did not find a monster or a place void of light. Surprisingly there was peace and a feeling of being no longer alone. In that moment I had ceased the fight with myself, and accepted all that was me, the good, bad, and the ugly. Somehow, within this acceptance of myself, I had touched some kind of soul purpose. Its picture broke the cherished view I had that life owed me answers. That its meaning is held somewhere other than in me.

You are never alone when you are at peace with yourself.

I was my own saviour and could no longer escape this. I created the meaning of my life by all that I thought and did. I had avoided this reality for the sake of making life easy. But it had not made it easy. It had only made me desperate and sad.

14

Evading this ultimate responsibility had only suspended my participation in life. It had taken away my inherent power of self-authenticity, the missing key to my freedom. A key I had misplaced somewhere in my youth.

This deep sense of self-responsibility gave me an unexpected truth; that there was no resource I could not find. No attitude I could not summon should I wish it to be so. That I could turn my will to any path, plant the seeds of any purpose, nurture any life within me that I chose. This idea was not new to me, but the power of it was now enormous.

Somehow in my search for something 'out there', I had forsaken myself. I had succumbed to the frenzy of the world and its illusion that I needed things. That I needed something that I did not have, needed to get or be something before I could be me.

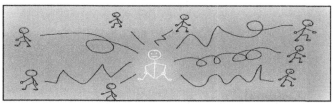

It was now clear that the dear parts of me that caused me grief were only doing what I (and the way of the world) had trained them to do. That my thinking, emotions, habits and other, apparently errant, parts of me were not malevolent, but servants. Parts of me that I was ultimately accountable for their training. I was not only the student and the teacher of me, but the God of what will and will not be in my life.

This degree of self-awareness and accountability was daunting. There were no more excuses. I could no longer blame myself for who I was. I was facing the responsibility of the all of me, the parts that I loved, and the parts I did not. It also made no sense to blame other people for how I was feeling, that was all just an avoidance. I was accountable for myself, the memories I held of life, and the way I thought and felt about today, tomorrow and my yesterdays.

I needed a robust, simple, useable understanding of the parts of me that do what they do. So, I set about distilling 35 years of knowledge and understanding into a simple picture that I could not dispute or avoid. A foundation that I could use for the rest of my life. The work of mapping out the apparent villainous and heroic parts of me was illustrated and explained in the book *The Sacred You – how to be your own saviour.* (Although a more earthy title would be *What the f*ck is going on and how to sort your shit out.)*

16

It was evident that I was not my thinking nor my emotions, or any of the other powers that were inherently human. They were servants; impartial faculties that responded to the forces that be, and the training I had given them. But the question remained: What were these servants there to serve? What was their purpose and what centre of gravity could summon their allegiance?

They did serve whatever I deemed important, whatever I had emotions about. My emotions power the mind and the stronger the emotions, (good or bad) the more my mind becomes preoccupied with it.

But my emotions were not consistent and often had little resonance to the deeper wishes I held for life. Their thousand voices all too often made my moment-by-moment decisions, at best, unpredictable and, at worst, calamitous.

So, I began the search to find a voice amongst the many that had my best interests at heart. The part of me that cared for my wellbeing and wished me well. It needed to have a power that could forge my will and the wit to cherish my integrity. It would be about courage, hope, fortitude, and above all, about love.

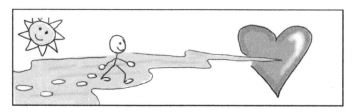

It was to the heart that I would travel, for the heart, is loyal to the soul of us.

But knowing the heart is no easy journey. Life can gather many vagrant emotions; unloved sorrows and strokes of anger, feelings that can bend the hearts meaning into shapes that carry no beauty, and certainly no freedom to the soul of us.

This journey to the heart would question the deeper aspects of my self-relationship, the love I held for myself. My love of me was not inclusive to all of me – I was a fair-weather friend to myself. There was a lack of humanity and kindness; the signs of my impatience, intolerance, and at times, outright hostility to myself were evident. I still had buttons that, when pressed, would change who I was being. Some I know: Monday mornings, old relationships, lack of money etc. But others could be pressed for no apparent reason; some unconscious something, the time of the month or even some obscure memory that decides to appear. So, I find myself in the company of the grumpy me who is pissed off at people or things, the sad me who is lost in an unresolved thread of remorse, or the angry me who has just had enough of everything.

But as this journey to the heart deepened, my tolerances changed. It was becoming increasingly uncomfortable to witness the hurt I was doing to myself. I was becoming less willing to erode my well-being with self-derision and blame, and no longer ready to abandon myself for the sake of just getting by in life.

To love yourself means
that it is OK to be you.

At the same time an awareness grew, of what seemed a sacred aspect of myself. It was of the heart, but far more than I imagined. It carried a peace, and a perception of life that was inclusive and loving. Whenever I was close to it, I was no longer struggling to see what could not be seen. It was as if I was touching the causal essence of things, a presence that dissolved the illusion that the nature of life was chaotic and without meaning.

What if there were somewhere within the heart, a place of peace and wonder, of wisdom and power? That is a light worth knowing.

So, I began the journey to know more of this benevolent part of me, to clear the path to my heart, and to learn to love myself.

Without heart, there is no meaning, no purpose-
no life!

IN THE BEGINNING

Real learning is not what we expect.

If we could expect it, it wouldn't be learning.

I looked in the mirror today and saw more than who I thought I was; within my eyes was a million years of purpose. I saw the depth of the universe and felt its unfaltering love. It was as if I had seen the divine within myself, the truth of who we are. The us that never dies, the custodian of our purpose, the love of our life.

This wasn't what I expected and was somewhat sobering. There was no blinding light, no sound of trumpets, and no big handshake with an almighty. But it was as profound as if there had been. For it seemed I was touching an eternal part of myself, an authority within that could create my heaven on earth, that was already *in* heaven on earth! It was a glimpse of something other than the me I thought I was. Its light questioned the lack of self-care and love I held for myself. And its presence would eventually crack and then dissolve my view of what I thought it meant to be human.

Doing a spiritual journey and tackling self-development issues can give many profound perceptions, and I have had my fair share of them. But this was different, this was personal. It was my eyes that were looking at me, something that I could not escape from. Could not be brushed off as a 'perhaps' or a nice perception that subsided over time. Its truth seemed to embed itself into my very soul.

What was in the eyes made it clear that there was something far greater in being human than I had assumed. A grace and sovereignty that was me, but so not-the-me I thought I was. Of course, I knew this stuff existed, but my mind always thought it was something that I was just not capable of being responsible for, that it was reserved only for the dream time.

The gentle threads that hold the meaning of life cannot be perceived by a hard mind.

My well-seasoned mind and clever thinking held little sway in this journey. Whatever it was, it was a heart thing, but a much deeper one than I had ever known. It dealt in knowings and senses of perception that were beyond what I was used to; outside of what I considered normal. To get anywhere close to this me that I loved, I needed a level of self-awareness that could only come from a sustained sense of self-care. It needed a commitment to my peace, to the soul of myself.

This would not be easy. I did care for myself and was pretty good at looking after my spiritual side. But this deeper self-care, that was tricky. I had my fair share of pain from life's experience; embedded feelings that caused attitudes that all too easily decimated my well-being and made me unmerciful to myself.

It was ultimately my lack of self-love that always eroded the communion with the heart of me.

We carry a thousand stories of who we are, some are loved, some are not.

Self-awareness and being on good terms with ourselves is something that we all care about, but taking this accountability into the depths of ourselves can be unnerving. We do avoid the deeper truth of our undesirable parts. It is easier to accept them as inevitable, an irrevocable consequence of life. So, we build behaviours to get by, hide, or even suppress them, but of course, they do not go away. They can't. They are us, the unloved parts of ourselves.

This lack of compassion and forgiveness to myself was now getting in my way of where I wished to go. And I couldn't drag these parts of me kicking and screaming into the future I now wished for myself.

I had to make amends with myself if I wanted to be with this, whatever-it-was that I felt within myself. So, I started, what seemed at the time, a monumental task of rebuilding my relationship with myself; to learn to love myself, so I might divine the divine within myself.

It was the heart that I sought if I was to love myself and it was the heart that I needed if I was to ever know again, the deeper truth that I had seen of me. The place of love, inspiration and courage. Qualities that I surely needed if I was to succeed.

The heart is the home of our heartfelt feelings of life, the living truth of who we are.

Simple really... but there was an entity in the way of this journey, a shapeshifter that was standing between me and this deeper aspect of my heart. It was elusive, over-sensitive, bloody-minded and often grumpy. It was the fragile me, a part of me that succumbed too easily to its fears and uncertainty. It held little trust in life or myself, and carried for its security, a vast list of preconditions and expectations of how life should be. And as life always turns out to be not what we expected, it is forever troubled!

Who do you think you are to write about these things? You have got to be kidding! No one wants to read your stuff, it's just dribble. And anyway, you've got no proper education, you can't spell, you're dyslexic and your grammar is crap. You're not really a writer. It's a fantasy. Every time you try to do it you know it feels impossible. You're just not strong enough, and wise enough, ha! What's the point anyway, you've never succeeded at anything really, it's just another waste of time.

To top this all off, this fragile self has been trained by a world that thinks that notions of the divine are silly and that learning to love oneself is a forlorn task, if not impossible.

It thinks it is happiest to stay within the comfort of the known, that to travel into the dark depths of ourselves is just too much trouble, that it is better to stay in the shallows of life for it does fear drowning.

This is the 'not very happy' companion on the journey to the heart. It is a voice of the mind, that vast complex array of energy and circuitry that gives us our arena of awareness, dominating what we see and do not see, what we feel and do not feel and, of course, what we think can and cannot be. In this task, it has at its disposal the vast subterranean sea that is the unconscious. A world that is filled with the years of our experiences and memories, that can often persuade us in ways that we do not understand.

This great unfathomable and, at times, errant part of us is the mind and is the mother of our beliefs; the feelings and meanings that tell us what should or should not be.

So, the first step of divining the divine of myself is self-awareness. It asks that I know, at least a little better, my own mind, the part of me which is both my greatest hero and, at times, the greatest villain in my journey to the heart.

A THOUGHT OF THE CHAPTER

Know thyself, for thyself is the crucible of the life, of what is and what will be.

Participation 1. *Our view of our self and the feelings we have because of it, can often seem out of our control; instigated by the chaos of life and the chaos of our self. This first exercise is to create a life line that can be used to help pull yourself out of places in yourself that you don't wish to be.*

Exercise: Create a self-affirmation. This exercise uses three questions to yourself to help bring clarity and action.

Step 1 – Find some time and place where you will not be disturbed for 10 - 20 minutes.

Step 2 – Gently quieten yourself and begin to let go of the noises that stop you being happy. This may be through meditation, song, dance, a walk in nature, or just sitting quietly.

When you have generated enough wellbeing that allows a sense of self care, ask yourself the following question.

How do I want to feel when I think about myself?

Create a strong sense of the feeling you want. It may have a colour, a sound or words. Keep it simple and feel the feeling you want.

When you have a resonant sense of how you want to feel about yourself, then ask yourself the following question.

How do I need to think about me to allow this feeling to happen?

28

You are now asking yourself for a new way of thinking that can get you where you wish to be. It is an affirmation of yourself for yourself; a set of words that activate the feeling that you want. These words need to be your own words, not someone else's.

Find a set of words that are simple and work for you. Finally write down the words you have created and repeat them to yourself often; especially when you are feeling strong. This will empower you. When you are feeling weak it will remind you to connect to love of self.

Participation 2. *We accrue many things as we go on in life, some useful, some not. The following exercise is a 'clutter clear' exercise to locate the core essentials that give you the most headway in your heart's journey in life.*

Exercise: Review your experience of life to distil the three core wisdoms, views of life and yourself that have helped you free the heart of yourself. They may be words that you create today, sayings you already use or stories that have always moved you.

1. _____
_____
_____
_____
_____
_____

2. _____
_____
_____
_____
_____

3. _____
_____
_____
_____
_____

When you have listed them, look to see what behaviour you do or can do because of them. Attitudes and actions that bring more of the truth of you into life.

_____
_____
_____
_____
_____

THE MIND

*A cloud will form according to the powers that be,
and when those forces change, so will the cloud.*

*The mind is the aura of presence created by our
memories, our thinking, our feelings, and the why
we do what we do.*

The mind seeks answers, the heart seeks communion.

The following sections on the mind are by no means comprehensive, the subject is vast and is not the purpose of this book, the heart is. But as our state of mind determines our relationship to our heart, I have extracted the aspects of the mind that are most prominent in our experience of it. By exploring these functions individually, we can place within them the story of ourselves as we experience them. By recognising aspects of the mind, we have a chance to separate it from the heart, and so understand our hearts intention more clearly.

I freely admit that this exploration of the mind and the heart is not founded on any scientific understanding, although it is likely to correlate with it. It is extracted from a lifetime of self-awareness and the sharing of personal experiences with those I have crossed paths with.

I have watched my mind for many years, and have witnessed with amusement, wonder, and at times horror at what and why it does what it does. Yet it is an ever-present companion and such a powerful part of our life; it holds not only our view of the world, but more importantly, our view of ourself!

The workings of the mind have been mused upon throughout the centuries, and thousands of beautiful writings have been created about it. But for most of us it can still remain a distant friend and, at times, an unruly partner. Yet the attitudes that it carries effect deeply what does and does not happen in our life. It is the home to our thoughts and the gatekeeper to the world. It can make a rainy day happy and a sunny day sad. This section on the mind is in five parts.

The relationship between thinking and emotions.

Feelings are the power that flows along the circuitry of associations I have about what I think goes with what.

Memories: How the mind uses memories to give life its narrative.

My memories are powerful and will bend the truth of what I see into shapes that fit the comfort of my assumptions.

How the beliefs that we carry constitute our Law of Attraction.

What I think because of what I see depends on the beliefs that are in residence at the time.

The reason why: The why-we-do-what-we-do is the power behind the act. They are the meaning in a look, the authority behind the words. *The why we do what we do may not always have words but, it will always have a feeling of a meaning.*

Will: How the mind uses willpower to enact the beliefs we carry.

Will is the part of the mind that chooses who I will be from the meaning I have about what I see and think.

THE MIND – THINKING & EMOTIONS

I do love my mind; it is one of the greatest faculties I have. It is a magnificent tool of perception, comprehension, and is a 'go-getter' of things. It holds the thousand threads to the places, people, and experiences of our yesterdays and the thousand threads to what may be in our tomorrows. It travels on the hopes and fears of our life. To places and times outside of the moment, to tomorrow's dreams and to yesterday's heroic moments and embarrassing disasters. It diligently searches through time and space to secure the answers to questions about what was, is, and what will be.

It is insatiably in its struggle to know things and will chase the How, Why, When, What and Where in its effort to find security in a world of constant change.

To distil meaning from the experiences of life, to define its place within the house of our mind by comparative analysis is what it does... all day long.

Thinking: *I am not my thoughts but my thoughts are a part of me.*

The thinking is the bridgebuilder of our associations; what we think goes with what. What we think about money, our partner, our work. What we think when we fail, and what we think when we look in the mirror.

The mind is a busy place; a moment does not go by without us thinking something. It's estimated that we have around 60,000 thoughts and make around 35,000 decisions each day. And with that, we accumulate thousands of emotions and feelings about what we have thought, seen or done.

The mind has been likened to an iceberg, where we see only the tip of it (the conscience mind) below which exists the vast mass of the unconsciousness. It is from this submerged part of us that much of our thought and action is drawn from. These hidden unconscious memories cause as much as 95% of our behaviour, an autopilot that is our habitual response to life experiences.

Yet our mind is also our point of consciousness of experience and where we make our meaning of life. The meanings we decide about our experiences of other people, a rainy day or what we decide our sadness means. These meanings, the why we say something then augments our picture of life. This picture then persuades the mind about who we are and how life is.

Our state of mind orchestrates the thinking, sending it down paths of rhyme and reason that belong to the meanings that our feelings give it.

Emotions: *I am not my feelings but my feelings are a part of me.*

Our thoughts of association, what we think goes with what, are powered by our emotions. The feelings that are created because of the meaning we put upon what we see and do. The stronger the emotions, the more powerful the association becomes. Our feelings tell the mind what is important to us. If we don't care it does not matter but if we do care it does matter. And the more we care, the stronger the emotion, the higher up the list of importance they go.

The mind is powered by our feelings. It will look to get more of whatever it is that our feelings are directing it to. If I am sad the mind will look for more things to be sad about, and if I am happy the mind will look for more happy things.

This emotional spiral will always get us more of whatever we are feeling. This is fine when we are in a good place but when I lose my balance and fall, my emotions will drag my thinking into places I would rather not go. My struggle then becomes to return to the solace of my heart, to find the compassion that can lift me from the dark caves of myself.

The mind seeks to define meaning for the feelings we have from what we see and think.

My mind is diligent in its attempt to gather more of what I am feeling. The trouble is I have feelings about so many things, often silly things, but because I have emotions about them my mind thinks them important. It then goes off to gather things to help define the feelings meaning.

This wandering of the mind is compounded by the world's persuasion that we be this or get that, making it difficult for the mind to settle. The emotions evoked by thinking we are missing out, that we need things we do not have to be happy, or feelings of being unworthy of the bright happy images in the media, this causes the mind to go chasing the things of life, things that all too often hold little meaning to the deeper purpose we wish our minds to hold.

But what if the forever rumblings of this and that, of what could or could not be is just an illusion of worth; a purpose that has no place of rest, no succour or light, only an endless separation from the soul of myself. What if this dark wish to secure and make safe the future, the next day, the next moment, makes me but a criminal in my stewardship to the moments of life?

Of course, the mind is only doing the job I have trained it to do; dancing to the tunes that my feelings have given it to play with. It is after all but a piece of consciousness that can only be conscious according to the remit that my feelings give it to play with. So, it is not really fair to blame myself for being who I do not like. Better that I understand my mind as a part of me that I am responsible to. Use care and forgiveness to help me help me. For I do care that my mind does not have to carry the burden of disunity, its weight inhibits my freedom and stops my mind from reaching the deeper dreams I hold of life.

*Our feelings are precious
they create our life of life.*

Our feelings are everything, they're the life force we are living. They are the point of our sentience of who we are being; they are what we are creating.

Our feelings are personal, two people may see the same sunset, but each carry away from it their own inimitable feelings of its meaning. These feelings we create from our experience are, like our fingerprints, unique.

They are our intimate story of life; an experience that we can never fully explain or express to others. We may sing a song about it, paint a picture of it, or even write a book upon it, but the actuality of the experience is always personal. It is ours alone, wrapped and perceived through the years of our experience. This aloneness that our uniqueness carries, is not a separation from life but our thread to its source, an intimate conversation with the soul of ourselves.

The mind will not easily surrender its grip on the fraction of reality that it has, for it thinks that that is all there is.

I once felt a bird in flight and saw as the bird sees, but that is rare, more often than not I see the bird and just think, 'that is a bird'.

The mind has worked diligently to create a secure world for us, a known world. It has many years of experience to build its perception of people, places and things, of what is and what should be.

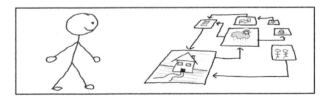

In its search for stability, the mind will name all things … as if it knows it all.

These embedded meanings about people, places and things create our expectations and conditions of life. Assumptions that can happily take us through the day naming all that we see.

That is a bird, that is a tree, that is a flower, a daffodil. That is an old person, that is a fat person, that is a pretty person. Today is a good day, a bad day. This moment is nice, not nice, better than the last moment and on and on.

This is the mind, declaring its opinion on all that it sees, as if it knows it all, as if all it knows is all that is.

This blatant naming of things has been created for our comfort. It does help navigate the day and do the things of life. But it is pervasive and imbued with habit, making it all too easy to settle into an ever-shrinking world composed of the same thoughts and same feelings about the same things we had yesterday. This would be ok if what I know was all that is but, that is far from the truth. We see only a fraction of the spectrum of life: there is a universe of life that exists beyond our current education and expectation; outside of the confines of our belief of what can and cannot be.

The trouble is every moment of the day, the mind is using the thinking and reasoning to build its narrative of the moments' meaning. They have become the predominant means of comprehension. From the moment we get up in the morning it's off, thinking this and reasoning that. It is unremitting and incessant, almost as if the mind fears oblivion if ever it was to stop thinking, as if thinking is all we are!

41

But this is not true. We live within a river of experience, a flow of life in every moment of the day, meanings from the feelings we get from each sound, colour and shape, and touch of life.

In a look, a lifetime can be seen; in a touch, the heart of another can be known.

We get feelings that carry meanings from a sunset, the sound of rain, the posture of another person or the laughter of a child. We are constantly getting a sense of life that is just too fast, too immense to be measured by thinking and reason; feelings that are beyond the scope of the conscious mind.

What if these great tools of thinking and reason are just inadequate in formulating this quest for the deeper truth of me? And what if I held, somewhere in the heart, that something that could read the truth of the moment, that could hold its presence and see its meaning?

Whatever I seek exists in realms beyond the collection of my memories. It requires something with the power and perception to see beyond the confines of my education, into the world of the soul of things for it is in the soul of things that the truth is always written.

42

A THOUGHT OF THE CHAPTER

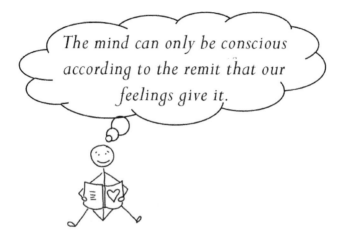

The mind can only be conscious according to the remit that our feelings give it.

THE MIND &
MEMORY

*Our memories create the window through which
we see the world, and the world becomes a
reflection of our experience.*

Our memories can plague us, entice us,
make us smile and make us cry. They
give us our strengths and our
weaknesses. They are an ever-present
influence that can be the cause of our
actions and decision in life. The bitterness, sadness
or guilt we carry will cause us to go down paths we
would rather not, and our ability to recover from
difficulty comes from times of gratitude we have put
into memory.

We hold memories from childhood, our teenage life
and adult life; millions of memories that are stacked
in the recesses of the mind, feelings of experiences
that can be evoked and into consciousness by a song,
a picture or even a smell. If we revisit places of our
youth, its memories will flood back as if it was
yesterday, as if that life of us still lives there.

We use our memories to get through the day. We could not get dressed, make a cup of tea, or find our way to work without our memories to show us the way. If I look around my home memories are everywhere, some hidden and some obvious. Each book on the shelves was an experience that gave me a feeling, and because of that a meaning that is held in my memory. The pictures on the wall, the objects on the mantel piece, the cup in my hands, they all hold a feeling of a meaning, however slight, that is held in memory.

Do not name the moment with your memories, it is so much more. Do not name yourself with your memories, you are so much more.

Our memories are the unspoken aura of ourself that make up who we think we are. A child has little thought of who they are because they have so few memories. They are unclouded by the conditions and expectations of memories and are able to laugh easily and love deeply. But the older we get the more memories we carry.

When I was young it was easy to remember what I loved but as I got older my struggle became to forget the memories of what I do not love.

This weight of memories can bend the truth of what we see into shapes that fit the comfort of our assumptions. They can take us through the day just living off the memories of all that we see.

Not seeing what we see, only seeing the meaning that was created yesterday. Like driving a car, it's easy to do, habitual; an unconsciousness that can be both bland and blind, where each person we meet and place we go is assessed and measured through the memories of our experience, a perception that may not be the truth but will be the truth we create. It may not be all that the moment is, but it will be all that we get from it.

When we let go of our memories, we enter the moments of the now, wherein a new sense of meaning becomes possible.

Our memories painting of the moment with the colours of yesterday's experience, is a second-hand view of life, a life outside of the moment's truth. But now and again memories hold on our perception becomes broken. Something, somehow gets past the wall of the conditions of life that our memory gives us, and we fall into a different place of our self. Perhaps from an inspiration or just a lucky moment; a reality that was always there, seeps out from behind the grey shapes, revealing a greater truth than the truth we thought was true. It can happen from a star-filled sky, a moment in intimate love or even in a shopping mall. A veil becomes lifted and a deeper sense of life is born, different to the one we have lived by.

When this happens, we get an insight into a soul's meaning of the moment; a meaning that is not beholden to our memories or our wish to satisfy the thought of who we are.

We abandon our attempt to define the moment's meaning, and become lost within the moment's cause. Uncoupled from our chain of thoughts we become blown away by some unreasoned truth, a feeling of a meaning that has no words. It is then that the sense of time dissolves, and we are no longer the witness to the moment's story, but its intimate companion.

This act of surrender separates us from the memories of who we think we are. And for that moment of time, we are more than who we thought we were. We slip into the company of the universe and become a part of all that we see.

All is now, now is all, all is OK.

The moment of the now is not perceived by thought or reason. We may, after its passing, use memories to compare it to other moments, to create a meaning, to decide what it means for us. But this is always a step away from the moment's truth, a fraction of the life of the moments meaning.

The actual moment itself is just too big, too wild to be contained by the words of the mind. It is life itself and has no comparison, no perceived outcome, no beginning and no end.

The willingness to be with the moment, without expectations, is the ultimate acceptance of life. It is a submersion into the unknown and a surrender to its timeless threads. It is where we can find our heart and fall back into love. It is where we find peace and where we can forgive. But these times of loved mystery are often fleeting, we can become drawn away from its journey by the wish to compare the incomparable; so, we think ourselves out of the moment, look to decide a meaning, give it a purpose that fits what is already known, what is already finite. In doing so we lose its living presence and assign it to the catacombs of memory. But the moment of the now is always there, it was there before we thought and will be there after we have thought. It is a living moment that exists outside of time. It has no season and no agenda. It is the crucible of life that is within every step and every breath we take.

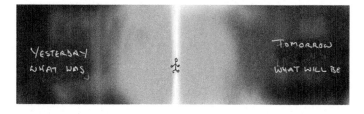

YESTERDAY
WHAT WAS

TOMORROW
WHAT WILL BE

It is where the soul can breathe. Unrestricted and undistracted, we become at home with the ineffable. And can be at peace with that, for there is no need to be anywhere else. It is love, for when we love we abandon our resistance to life, we enter its flow and become a part of all that we see, and all is well.

The why we do what we do will either come from our memories or from inspiration, one will bring the dark, one the light.

In my wish for freedom, it is memories that cloud the way. They make assumptions that belittle life's beauty and hide the beauty of myself. When I respond with some soggy, troubled memory, the shit hits the fan, but whenever I respond from inspiration, it is always extraordinary, and that is the freedom I seek.

Our memories may paint our picture of the day but the actual moments of life will always be more than our memories can give it.

THE MIND & THE REASON WHY

You can hit a drum with a thousand different attitudes. The drum's sound will carry its meaning exactly as it was struck. Yet it is not the drum, but the reason why it was struck that counts; for without the reason, the drum has no purpose.

The mind does not pay attention to what we are thinking, it listens to why we are thinking it.

 Behind the chatter of the thoughts of each day, exits the reason of why we are thinking them. This 'why' may not always have words but, it will always have a feeling of a meaning.

The why-we-do-what-we-do is the power behind the act; the meaning in a look and the authority behind the words. It is the underlying motive of our action and reaction to what we see and do. It is the deeper truth of who we are being.

The 'why' we do what we do is the primordial meaning of ourselves that exists below the chatter of our thoughts.

Our 'why' is the measure of our true worth, because it is always not what we do, but why we do it that counts. It is the meaning we are living and giving.

It is this truth of ourselves that the mind uses as an understanding of who we are. They become the flags that identify to the mind our deeper purpose, and the mind is duty bound to support it; to gather and bring 'more' of its associated meanings, thoughts and feelings.

We can't always choose what we do. but we always have the choice of why we do it.

Our first option of choice is in *what we do,* but this is often governed by life's necessities and our choices can be limited. The second option of choice is in *how* we do what we do, what attitude we apply to what we do. Our choice here is easier to claim although the *how* is often driven by habitual behaviour, making it a struggle to bring our consciousness into the process. The final point of choice is in the *why* we do what we do. This is always within our grasp and if we do not claim it, it will also be claimed by our habitual response. But this 'why' is the most powerful. The *why* we do what we do, impacts deeply on the *how we do what we do.* And when we bring our consciousness to the *why* we do things it can often changes the *what* we do.

The 'how' we do what we do determines the kind of 'what' that happens, and the 'why' we do what we do determines what kind of 'how' we use in 'what' we do.

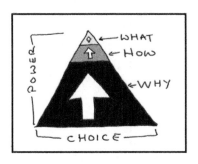

In the thousand acts we do each day; each will have behind them a why-we-do-it.

Why we get up in the morning; why we go to work; why we give a smile to another: these will all have a feeling that is drawn from the beliefs we have at the time. Good days will have reasons that come from positive beliefs and bad will have bad. Our reasons will form according to the colour of our beliefs at the time.

Whatever this day means for you is your choice.

You may give it any meaning that you want.

It may not change the day but it will change you.

We can change our mind, change the beliefs it is carrying, by changing the reasons why we do what we do. I can clean the house because it is dirty or because I want the freedom a clean house gives. I can leave the house to go to work because I do not have enough money, or I can change my belief about money by changing the reasons why I do it; go to work for the purpose of creating greater opportunities that money can give.

The 'why's' we use in a day create the mind's palette and these colours and their feelings then orchestrates the thinking. Our thinking then becomes the manifestation of their unspoken persuasion.

This critical power of self-creation, the 'why' we do what we do is more than just an idea, it is our claim to life. It tells life 'Who' we are, and the power of life gives us full measure in return. But this profound source of our life can be elusive to call our own. It can easily be abandoned to a suspect morality, a social conformity, a parental voice, or even a religious doctrine that can give us 'oughts' or 'shoulds' that carry no hearts meaning. The 'why' we do has also been terribly usurped by consumerism and the media that tell us what we should want, all that we should be, to be worthy of their pictures of life.

When I feel into the why I do what I do; look to see where it is coming from. I can see that some whys are kind to me and some are not. I have noticed that they change according to how far away I am from the heart of me.

When we are in touch with our heart, the why we do things comes from gratitude, care and with forgiveness; because of love. But when we are away from the heart, it is all too easy for our reasons to be prompted by fear; fear of losing what we have or fear of not getting what we think we should have.

When I allow fear to create my reasons, it does darken the mind. A sense of unworthiness easily appears, a mirage that causes me to chase what can never be found with fear, the peace of me. So, I end up lost in the lonely story of myself.

But when I bring my consciousness to my acts, feel the meaning that I am living. I can see where its consequences will take me. This helps me shift the primary cause of my acts away from the darker shades of fear, into the lighter meanings of love.

Much of this inner journey seems to be an ongoing awareness of how close I am to love and how much I have let go of fear.

We may always choose the reason for what we do, decide its purpose, and create its meaning. This 'why' is the ultimate tool of our self-definition.

Participation 1. *Morning pages was created by Julia Cameron and is a great exercise for clearing the mind, generating ideas and having less anxiety. It is a way to slow down the mind and to find out how you are. This can build a great friendship between you and the mind.*

Exercise: Spend time writing down a few pages of your thoughts each morning. Just write what's going through your head without judgment or censure. It does not have to be intelligent or profound, just the thoughts as they arise, or just a good ramble.

Participation 2. *Having a 'go to' list of things that help swing the balance of our mind, away from a malign into a benign view of the world is a great asset. I often do some housework to help clutter clear my mind, or some gardening to get back to the earth. A mediation always helps. An inspiring or funny movie will always help lighten the load.*

Exercise: This is a 'know thyself' exercise. Make a list of things that you do or can do that you know bring back a greater belief in the gift of life. Put the list in a prominent place in your home to help you remember to remember.

Participation 3. *Why we do what we do does program the unconscious mind, and the choice of Why is always ours. By creating a motive for our actions that fits to who we love to be, and then locking it into a repetitive habit, we can create a positive power-source for ourselves.*

Exercise: Choose one or two habitual actions, making a cup of tea, opening a door, getting into the car, getting dressed, anything that you do on a daily basis. Then create your own conscious reason for doing it, a reason that cares for your well-being.

Participation 4. *We live in a very 'head' based culture with much thinking. this can leave little time to recognise and respond to our heart's feelings. The flowing practice helps to develop trust and listening to the heart. It also reminds you that you want to know the hearts guidance.*

Exercise: Make one conscious decision each day that uses the heart rather than the head. It may be what you want to do this day. Where you will go for a walk. Who you want to talk to or even what part of your house needs your attention and care. This exercise may require you to sit quietly for a few minutes as you move from the head to the heart, from a thinking to a feeling perception.

Participation 5. *The way of the world can often make important things unimportant and unimportant things important. This can leave us chasing things we do not need and forgetting what we truly love.*

People who have near death experiences nearly always go through this exercise. Their life and their time become crucial and their priorities change.

The following exercises is to consciously recreate your priorities; the top things you really don't want to live without, actions and attitudes that bring happiness and help create the best of you.

You can start at the top and then work down as a list, or do a brain storm or mind map. The purpose is to remind yourself what you truly care about. It may be people that you care about, or activities that you love.

Exercise: Create a hierarchy of your importance's. The core things you would not want to live without.

THE MIND – WILL

 Although I do long for a will that is steadfast to my purpose, inviolate to the tides of time and resolute in the face of life's turmoil, I am not sure it's fair for me to think that it could, or should be. Sometimes life can be, and is, a why-bother kind of day…'

I am just not in a good place in myself to write… I seem to have misplaced my will. It's not where it usually is and its absence has caused my strengths to drain from me. I have forgotten a dream I held of who I am and find myself rummaging the unholy desert of myself. I have become unwilling to nurture hope's' company and she has duly departed. So, I find myself stirring the troubled water of myself; and in doing so, have awoken the unkind parts of me.

When these days happen, the test of my will becomes how little harm I do to myself because, like all things, this too shall pass.

It is by our will that we maintain our integrity and with that, our authenticity.

There is no roadmap given at birth. Nobody showed us how to create our heaven on earth. We had to make it ourselves, create a purpose and choose the meanings that drive our life. Then, through the power of our will, muster our heart and mind towards its end.

Will is our power of choice; the power of action that creates what will and will not be. Some acts are big and need great willpower, but many are small and happen throughout the day; whether we will smile at another or not, choose tea or coffee, stay in bed for another ten minutes, or whether we will go for a walk or watch TV. Our will is always present. It is our path chooser; our path creator. Without it we would have no response to life, make no decisions, have no choice.

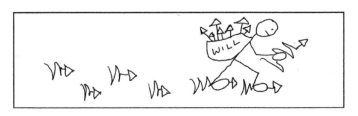

Whatever our will, it needs to have the true colours of ourself. No second-hand or borrowed will can suffice. Another's will is just not strong enough, not prudent enough to create the path of our self. It is, after all, our will, our distinct touch in life. It is sacrosanct and should not be given away. But like the person, who left their heart's purpose to become what the parents wanted of them, it is all too easy to break our integrity and abandon the true story of ourselves.

The hard will learns the tune and the soft will sings the song.

Some days I need a hard will that can drive me forward or to dig myself out of the hole I have fallen into. And some days I need a soft will that allows me to just love the moment.

The hard and soft will are our creative powers- the will to do into the outer world and the will to perceive the inner world.

The Hard Will, by its nature, is inflexible, and narrow in its focus. It deals primarily with the manifest and has little perception of the forces that cause the known world to be. It is the will to do, and the will to resist that which stops the doing. It makes safe the place of our creations. I am grateful for my hard will; without it I would never get out of bed in the morning. It has drive and focus. It loves the practical and utilises the thinking and reasoning to build its 'to do' list. It is a great doer and with all its bluster, noise and action, it is much admired and sought after in the world today. Those demonstrating its ability are well rewarded with money and power.

The hard will is great for getting there but not so good at 'being there'. The 'being there' is the domain of the soft will.

The trouble is my hard will suffers from overrun. It gets twitchy and insecure with the 'being there' bit. This often makes life an endless 'getting there' with very little 'being there'. But the hard will to make the path and clear the way is only half the story of our will.

The Soft Will catches knowing's that exist at the edge of our perception. It has the ability to connect to the creative force of life and to see beyond the confines of our assumptions. It is open, flexible and has an agility that perceives the living meaning of things. And because of that, the ability to connect and create from the causal essences of life.

I can find the soft will often after a meditation, sometimes in a walk in nature or just with a lucky moment. It emerges whenever I let go of my 'to do' list or my expectations and conditions of the moment. When I manage to do this, it joins me to my heart, whose presence carries no fear, only flavours of gratitude and a dash of the awe of life. It is then that I can catch the greater truths of life and the inspiration for its journey.

The soft will is a gentle dance of perception.

Its way is a contemplation.

A meditation without conditions.

A gratitude that has an unhurried journey into the unknown.

It seeks love and so, listens to the forces that wish us well.

It asks only that we trust, at least in this moment, that all is well.

Our greater will is always to be true to ourselves, to have the courage to be who we wish to be and the grace to accept who we are.

Participation – Beyond Thinking & Reason

Participation 1. *Life is busy, there is always things to do, to fix, to find out. But all the doing can often become a burden that we never put down. This exercise is to help bring back a balance to the cut-and-thrust of life. It is a soul breathing exercise to find the freedom to heal from just being, to feel the moment without conditions or expectations.*

Exercise: Present moment awareness. This may be something that you already do in meditation but allow some time in a day, when there is no distraction, to just be with the moment. Bring your awareness to the body, gently feel the air, feel the breathing of the lungs. Count each breath and when your thoughts have taken you out of the moment, start the count again. Sit through the urge 'to do' as an escape from any sense of boredom that may arise. Give yourself a break and allow your thoughts to come and just go. For a few moments, just be, and allow life to pass you by as you find yourself again.

Participation 2. *The first exercise was about being happy in the moment, this exercise is about owning and learning from our negative emotions. The feelings and emotions we have are our power, they show us who we are being and create who we are. When our feelings are negative, perhaps because of what someone said or did or even when we are just having a grumpy day,* *the mind will often go into a frenzy of thinking and reasoning to fix it. It will look to assign fault or blame as a means of resolving the feeling. Or even blaming ourselves as an escape of ownership.*

Our feelings carry a meaning. Many negative feelings are created from some hurt within us. If we are able to listen to that feeling, become aware of what it is saying to us, we have a chance to escape its cycle.

Of course, there will always be something else that is more fun to relieve the pain we feel, but now and again allowing what is simply to be what is, gives time for the meaning within the feeling to show us the way through of the hurt. And that is always the greater healing.

Exercise: Now and again, choose a time to accept your negative feelings. Give them their time without thinking it through, without crushing them or rushing to dissolve or resolve them.

THE MIND — BELIEFS

To be aware of our belief and to be willing to decide afresh whether they are wise is good housekeeping.

 Beliefs are the clustered memories and feelings we have from life's experience. They give us views on life and ourselves. Views that may not be true but they are what we believe.

Our beliefs create motives for many of our acts and our will is its inevitable manifestation. We will not climb a mountain without the belief that we can, and we will not succeed without a good reason for doing it!

Although some beliefs are created consciously with logic and reason, many beliefs are not. They can be inherited. I know a person whose mother was badly treated by the Russians in the second world war. The mother's hatred of the Russians was then passed to her daughter. She now has an instant dislike for anyone speaking Russian.

We also get beliefs from our impressionable youth: A comment from a teacher that you can't paint can cause an indelible feeling of failure where doing art is concerned. I had a tough experience at school that made a belief that I was useless at writing. This created a whole pile of thinking, this is impossible! I can't do this! that I had to wade through, whenever I sat down to write.

Some beliefs can be created from times of pain. My father's mother died because she was a Jehovah witness and refused blood when ill. His trauma of her death created an aversion and hostility to religions ever after. Beliefs can also be Indoctrinated into us by religion, government, social conformity and of course the media.

These embedded emotions interpret our experiences. If we are in a belief of being a victim, we will read our experiences accordingly; believe that people and things are 'out to get us' and so become closed and defensive. If we believe that life owes us a living, we will look to see what we can take and will become unwilling to give, and of course, if we believe that life is a gift, we become open to its opportunities.

Whatever beliefs are active, exudes their stored feelings, these then become the centres of gravity for the thinking. This will, in turn, create more feelings that deepen existing beliefs. It is a self-perpetuating cycle that is compounded by our experiences of life and the thoughts we have about it.

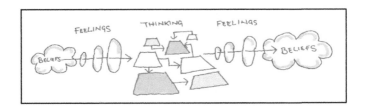

This is the great machine the that holds together our picture of reality, a world that is made from the thousands of beliefs we have of ourselves and life.

If we rely on other people and things for our self-belief, we will always be at the mercy of the weather of the day.

Our consciousness does make us aware of ourselves, and according to our feelings at the time, creates a view of who we think we are. This self-identity gives us the beliefs about what we can and cannot do. What we feel we are worthy or not worthy of.

Although we can have constant beliefs about things like a football team, political parties, the opposite sex, money, authority, or even the existence or not of God, our belief about ourselves is rarely constant. They can change according to what other people think of us, the size of our bank account, whether the sun is shining, or even if we have cleaned the house or not.

This unstable ground that we try to build our self-belief upon gives the mind an impossible task, to find security in the world of constant change.

We can have different thoughts about the same thing, at different times, according to the self-belief we have at the time. When we are feeling good about ourselves, the day's tasks are easy to do, but when we are feeling low, they are a struggle to accomplish. When life's experience dissolves our self-belief, it does evoke the sense of fragility. Our view of life changes, it becomes harder and darker. We doubt ourselves and so, meet a part of us that is in trouble, is in need of healing. These times are always a challenge to our life, do we avoid it or are we able to take the next step in our self-development.

The well of gratitude that we create in times of wellbeing, does give nourishment in times of self-doubt.

There are many things we can do that help maintain a healthy self-belief: Having fewer attachments, creating boundaries, making times for self-nourishment, doing self-affirmations, and eating well and exercise. But the question still remains, where can we find a self-belief that can withstand the inevitable chaos of life?

Creating and maintaining a positive self-belief that is not beholden to other people and things, is one of the toughest tasks we can ever do. It has caused me to drive deep into myself, to know and heal the causes of my suffering. It has also created a deep wish to know my heart, as it seems to be the source of my true happiness.

The mind's belief of ourselves forever changes but the heart's belief of ourselves is incessantly constant.

Many of the following chapters are this journey and are the stepping stones I have used to know what my heart already knows.

A THOUGHT OF THE CHAPTER

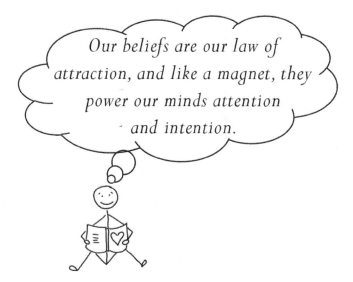

Our beliefs are our law of attraction, and like a magnet, they power our minds attention and intention.

THE UNKNOWN

There is life beyond our belief, outside the confines of our expectations, and the conditions we put upon how things should be.

My arrogance avails me of no truth or peace, for the gentle threads that hold the meaning of life cannot be perceived with the hard mind.

A story – There was a man who lived in a house, in a street, in a town. Every day he would have breakfast of toast and marmalade. It was always toast and marmalade and it was always tea with one sugar. After breakfast, he would go for a walk in the park. He would follow the same path and see the same trees as he had always done. There were other paths in the park but he always walked the same path. He had done it for years and knew it well. He would sit on the same bench that he always did and feed the birds with the bread that he always put in his pocket before he left home.

One strange morning, he looked at his marmalade, toast and his cup of tea he wondered if he might like something different to eat. But he couldn't think of anything else, so he ate his toast and drank his tea and went to the park as he always did, but this day he felt confused at the juncture in the path. He always took the left path but today he was not sure. He felt he wanted to take the right path, but that was ridiculous, he always took the left path and anyway that was where his bench was, that was where he fed his birds.

So, he took the left path. As he was sitting on his bench, feeding the birds he wondered where the right path would lead to and if he should have taken it. OK, he thought to himself, tomorrow I would take the right path to see what's there. The next day as he approached the choice of path in the park, he became unsure. Will there be a bench there?

Where will I feed the birds? There were just too many questions he did not know the answer to. I will take the right path tomorrow he thought and so, took the left path. But tomorrow came and he never took the right path, nor the day after or the day after that. And he never found out what was at the end of the other path.

What if this fear of treading on uncertain ground, of stepping too far is just subjugation upon the soul of me? That my wish for certainty and its illusion of safety does no justice to the glory of life and only violates the heart of who I am?

It does need courage to bring our dream to earth. It is to go on our own creative journey and that is always a journey into the unknown.

This journey to the heart and soul of me was defiantly out of my ordinary. It took me to the hidden realms of myself, to places where my badges of 'spiritual' accomplishments were of little use. To places where the light I had nurtured all my years offered limited guidance.

I had to let go of my self-view, a view that bound me to a known world, and enter the solitary realms of my uncharted self.

I was to trust a journey where no path was visible and believe that the unknown of me bore me no ill will.

As the self-images I had made for security crumbled, it became obvious that the views I had of myself were simply not true. That not only was this 'who I thought I was' inadequate, but also misleading. My need for security had forced me to live with conditions that offered little belief in the vast unknown of life. It had made me seem an orphan in a world without colour, while the real truth of me was wildly different. I was a home unto myself and held within me, the infinite world of colour.

We are more precious than we know,
more powerful than we believe,
and more loved than we can ever see.

But stepping into this greater dream is not easy. It is beautiful, but also unknown. It was outside of an ordinary that a part of me finds comfortable and secure. So, in my quest into the unknown, I often find myself dragging a bruised and sulky self. A part of me that is unhappy at adventure because of the self-harm I do when things don't go as expected.

My dear mind does like to calculate stuff. To know what will be, and how things will turn out, and what it can get from its adventures. But you can't calculate the unknown, it is... unknown.

Can the experience of a wild dance be known before it happens? Can the maestro know the beauty that they will create when they first touch the instrument? Do the innocent eyes of the child know the years of life before them? And can the incredible journey of love with another be known at its first glance?

This is a journey with no guarantee, only the certainty of no regret. It is a journey of no return, for although we can pretend that we may go back to the way things were, to be cosy in the acceptance that normality is all that is. The truth is it's not possible. Normal will inevitably become inadequate, unable to hold the truths that will be found in the heart of you.

There is one thing I am certain of: there is more to life than I know.

A story: There was a boy who lived in a world without colour. It was not dark and it was not light it was a half-light, a grey light. Everything was grey, his room was grey, the sky was grey, the trees were grey, even the flowers were grey. It wasn't a bad grey; it was just grey and he was tired of the grey. It had always been grey, it's all he could remember. But there was a part of him, a little part of him that that seemed to know of something other than grey. As if there was, once upon a time, some kind of colour.

Each day, when he opened the window and looked out into the grey garden, that part of him that seemed to know of colour, would expect to see it somewhere in the garden. But that was silly, it had always been grey. So, each day the grey world would just look back at him and the part of him that seemed to know of colour would be sad at the sight of the grey. But he never lost hope. And each night as he went to bed, he held onto this part that seemed to know about something other than grey.

One night, after he shut his eyes to the grey world he began to dream, and in his dream, he saw something other than grey! It was colour! And it was beautiful! Small flashes of colour at first. There were little bits of red and a beautiful green. There was also a yellow, such a lovely yellow and he was sure he saw some orange. It was wonderful and during the following nights the flashes of colour in his dreams became bigger, stronger and brighter. It wasn't long before his nights became a dazzling dance of colour. And each morning, he wished that somehow there was some way that the colours of his dreams could spill into the grey light of his day. But each day the grey world would be there, as grey as ever.

One morning, instead of opening his eyes when he woke up, he kept them closed and staying in the half-dream of the beautiful lights, he began to imagine the garden covered in colour. In his mind, he painted the flowers, the trees, the sky, and the sun with the beautiful greens, yellows, reds and blues of his dreams. He kept this picture in his mind and slowly, very slowly opened his eyes.

This time when he looked out into the garden, he thought he saw some colour. He rubbed his eyes, was he dreaming or was it real.

When he opened his eyes again it was still there. It was real. There was some colour! Just the slightest strokes of colour in the flowers and the trees but it was there.

It was his garden but like he had never seen it before, it was alive! He ran out into the garden to get close to the colours but they began to fade, for after a while he lost the memory of the dream and the strokes of colour in the trees and the flowers drained away.

Each morning he tried, again and again, to hold the colour of the dream and paint the picture of the garden. And although there would often be small bits of colour, it would always fade back into the grey again. He must try harder he thought. So, the next morning he tried as hard as he could to paint the picture and remember the lights. He struggled so much that he was sure that the colour would be there and stay. But this time when he looked out of the window, there was no colour at all! There was not even a hint of the colours he had seen before. It was all just grey.

What had gone wrong? He had tried as hard as he could. He felt empty and so alone without the colours His eyes filled with tears. He didn't know what else he could do to bring back the colours to the day.

But that little part of him that seemed so certain of the colours would not go away, it would not let him give up! So, each morning before he opened his eyes he wished as hard as he could to see the colours in the day.

He wished and wished and wished until he had no more wishes left to give but still the colour was nowhere to be seen. The grey half-light had returned forever.

But he still had his dreams. So, each night he went to sleep happy to dream of the colours and the light.

One morning, before he opened his eyes, while he was still waking up and still surrounded by all the beautiful colours. He decided to just keep the feeling that he got from seeing the colours. Regardless of the grey that was waiting for him, he would get up holding onto the feeling he had in his heart from the colour of his dreams.

So, he got up as usual but this time keeping the feeling of being covered in colour. He went to the window, expecting the grey to be there, as it had always been. But this time there was some colour, quite a lot of colour. The trees seemed greenish, the sky blueish and each of the flowers had some lovely little bits of colour.

He smiled so deep to see the colours again. And there were so many colours to be seen, the greens in the grass, the greens in the trees.

Then there were the flowers, what colours they had, pinks, yellows, reds, oranges and bright whites. It seemed as if everything was dancing in colour.

As he watched the dawn of this wonderland, he did not let go of the feeling inside of himself, for he noticed that the stronger the feeling, the brighter the colours became. And they did become brighter, the sky became a blanket of blue.

It was so blue it took his breath away. And then there was the sun, what a sun it was. A big beautiful yellow and orange sun that seemed to give life to all the colours. He had never seen the world like this before and he danced and sang full of joy of the colours.

As he danced it rained, like silver, and then he saw the greatest wonder of his life, the rainbow! What a sight it was, it filled the sky and his heart with the beautiful song of its colours.

From that day on, each morning, he held close to his heart, the feelings that he wanted to see in the day, he kept it simple and he kept it safe.

There were a few greyish days to come but most were filled with colour, bright, strong colour, and such joy.

The heart knows what the mind cannot see.

There are times when I find myself standing on the edge of precipice between who I was and who I wish to be. Times when the great unknown of me just seems too much. It is then that I often hear a voice that urges me forward.

With the brave of me shall I build a fire
and I shall give to the pyre all the memories of who I
was; all that I have been and all the stories of what
was and what was not.

I shall grieve no tears to dampen the fire,
but stoke it more with all that I am
and all that I think I shall be.

So, I may go home again and breathe
the impossible once more.

A THOUGHT OF THE CHAPTER

The freedom we seek is nurtured in the mystery of life and in the acceptance of the mystery of ourselves.

Participation 1. *There is a wealth of life beyond our prepared knowledge of things; outside of the confines of what we think is true.*

The following exercise uses the heart instead of the head as a way of understanding. It is a process that develops trust in the hearts ability to know the unknown. This is an art of patience, to understand what the mind cannot see. It can be applied to times of trouble as well as times of joy. This practice needs to be done with no perceived outcome and no expectations.

Exercise: Sit in front of a flower or a tree for 10 minutes. Be without judgment or expectations. Get past the wish to give it names, to tell it what it is, and gently keep your focus on it. Sense it as it is, not what you think it should be.

Participation 2. *The mind does like to know things, to organise and have a plan, and has a hundred conditions of how it thinks things should be. The following exercise is to play without expectations or conditions of how things should be.*

Exercise: Relax in the unknown you. Spend 15 minutes doodling with no known purpose, allow the pen to explore the page. (What is drawn does not have to make sense or even be pretty.)

Participation 3. *Just as our mind likes to express itself with words, so does the body with dance. The following exercises uses this wish to explore our inner rhythms and our creativity. It is an exercise to allow your feelings of the body to be expressed in movement.*

Exercise: Dance with no music. Feel the rhythms within your body and express these in movement. Start by just moving your arms and then allow the whole body to join in.

THE HEART

In bringing the heaven that is held within our heart to earth, we fulfil the promise we made for this lifetime.

When we go with our heart, it is always an adventure, a trusting in an unfathomable thread. When we can do this, we become the hero of ourselves. We remake our life with the indisputable truth: the heart of us.

This chapter is now focusing upon the very heart of this journey and this book. And although expressions 'to speak from the heart', 'hand on heart', 'have a heart', 'put your heart into it' are common, the actuality of our own heart is not so intangible. It is not a head thing and can't be calculated. It is felt. So, I have used poetic licence more often here to bring about a feeling rather than a thinking perception. Although, there are activities at the end of the chapter that will help discern its meaning as an objective and personal understanding.

There is within ourselves, a dream we carry for this life; a knowing and a wish that is faithful to a greater vision of ourselves. It is our heartfelt feeling of love about life and our story within it. Its actuality is known only by ourselves and it is only we who can give it the light of day.

Of all the subjects within this work, the picture of this one is the hardest to paint. It is elusive to know yet it is what we live for. It is the gentlest of things and also the most powerful. It cradles our love and also holds the struggles of our journey.

Its importance has been known for thousands of years and spoken about in stories, fables and mythology. To *follow your heart* is the constant message, and to *speak from the heart* is always a turning point in the story.

The heart is at the heart of the human journey, yet its profundity is hardly recognised. Its image has been abused by the media and overused by the well-meaning, reducing its life of passion to an 'ought' or 'should'. But the real heart is no place of shallow emotions or vain morality; feelings that can masquerade as a heart's meaning. It holds no imitation of truth, no charade of meaning. It has something far more within it.

It is a door to something greater than any bland education can cope with. It is the home of a benevolent will, of courage, of a relentless compassion and an infinite hope. It is the source of our love and has the power for loves embodiment. It is the saving grace of humanity, because for every heartless act in the world there are hundreds of acts of heart; of care, of kindness and of love.

This deep heart seems to live in a different world than the one I am used to; a timeless world that has within it, images that make the brash brushstrokes of my mind seem childish by comparison. Its truth is subtle and each time I sit down to write about it, I feel like a fumbling giant trying to pluck the most delicate of flowers.

But I know that within the heart exists the greatest companion and my dearest friend. So, I let go of the hundred things of the day, and slowly my centre of gravity shifts as I become pulled into a different realm of myself.

It is a chamber of the miraculous and the source of well-being that fits like a glove to who I am. It is the me that knows why I am here; the remembrance of some lost forgotten vow I made for this life.

A song without heart carries no life.

It is from the heart that comes so many defining qualities of love and the human adventure of life. It is the source of our abiding happiness, because the wish of the heart is for our happiness. It knows what is best for us because it knows us intimately. Within its chamber lives our loves, hopes, and our dreams.

The heart is the source of all the world's greatness. It can pull star dreams to earth, for the heart has created all the wonders of the world, all the gifts of humanity and all the songs of love. It is the home of an innocence, a wise innocence that dispels the cynicism I hold in myself and of myself.

It is the place of our truth, not the truth of yesterday or tomorrow that my mind struggles to know, but the truth of the moment, the living truth. And when I allow it, it is a cathedral of light, a library of illumined text that describes the union of my heaven and earth. Its call has the power to move mountains or create the gentlest touch of love. It is the artist within, the writer of meanings, and the manifestor of dreams.

Although we live in a world of this-and-that, there is within the heart the dreams of forever and memories of the infinite.

The following story appeared whilst I was sitting in a cathedral admiring its special space.

In times past, it was not possible for the human to perceive their direct connection to God, so the great temples and churches with all their beautiful images and architecture were created as houses of God and offered as a mirror to the place within ourselves where this was possible, our own heart.

The priests and holy people became the stewards of God until such a time as humans were able to know their own hearts. These houses of God and places of worship, became the home for guidance, succour, and relief from the apparent absence of God.

Although this was useful it did compound the illusion that the divine aspect was outside of us and that it was them not the people that could know God.

That atmospheric glory and peaceful beauty that the great temples and cathedrals have held within their walls is but a meagre reflection of what can be found within the chamber of our own heart. The door is now open, and it only asks that we cherish our life above all else, for when that cherishment is true it will be given to all that we see.

This is my quest to divine the divine within myself, dowsing for God if you like.

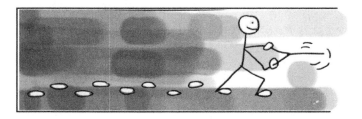

The heart is the source of our truth, not the truth of yesterday or tomorrow that the mind struggles to know, but the truth of the moment, the living truth.

Participation 1. *We have to do much head work living in this world, much thinking, sorting and reasoning to cope with the demands of work, paying bills, housekeeping, dealing with family and the thousand day-to-day bits we to do to just get by. This has made the head the predominant 'go to' place for perception and action. This has made the mind the master and the heart its servant. Of course, this is the wrong way round, and has left the hearts faculty of perception as second best, or just an emotional luxury we haven't got time for.*

The following exercise is a reflective and listening exercise. It is about communing with the heart, and learning to value its love and wisdom. It is also, a reminder to yourself that you do care what is in your heart.

It is best done after loosening the minds expectations of the moment with a meditation, a walk in the countryside or even quiet time in a comfy chair.

Exercise: Bring your attention to your heart space, be there for a while and then ask yourself, what does your heart know that your mind cannot see? You can ask your heart about something that the mind has been bothered about or just an open invitation for the heart to let you know something it cares about. Write, draw or even sing a song from its response.

_____

_____

_____

_____

_____

_____

_____

_____

Participation 2. *We are made up of many different lives and our heart is an important one. How we feel and communicate with the parts of our self, determines what we allow them to give us. The following exerciseis to let the heart know that you care for it.*

Exercise: Write a love letter or poem to your heart. It doesn't have to be perfect, only heartfelt. It can be a gentle ramble, wild scribbling, a few words or even a drawn image.

_____

_____

_____

_____

_____

_____

_____

Participation 3. *Words are powerful and the words we use define our world. Out of all the words that you know, what are the most important for you, what words hold your love and passion of life? Words that bring an inner smile, evoke values that stir your heart, that bring you peace?*

They are your unique collection of words that form a picture of your love. The following exercise can be done before, and then again, after a mediative time to give two levels of self-awareness.

 Exercise: Write your favourite words within the heart.

KNOWING THE HEART

The struggle to live from our heart, to be and speek the truth of ourselves, is not a casual thing. It is the prophond journey of being human. A purpose that has been carried for thousands of years.

Where are we drawn back to after the storms of life hit us, when chaos drives out our careful plan? Where do we find hope when the trials of life just get too much? What paths can we make, what signs have we created to see the journey home, to re-join the conversation with our beloved self?

It will be our heart, for it is the home of the dream we would not want to live without. It holds our passion, our purpose, and our love. It is the source of our true song, and because of that, our comfort and our freedom. But how easily can we find this place that can give peace to the troubled mind and soothe the soul.

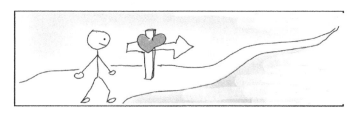

The heart's presence is never absent. Sometimes it is drowned out by the demands of life, and sometimes; trodden on by our own exasperations. But even in life's cacophony, it will always be with us. It is, after all, the heart of us. The evidence of its wish can be seen throughout our life. From childhood to this day, there are signposts that allow us to know our heart's intention. Irresistible actions and creativities that, in their adventure, have shown us love, given joy, and created peace.

If I look through the history of my life, at the appearance and flavours of my loves. I can see a thousand loves, insatiable desires that have always been there. These times of passion and inspiration were not arbitrary. They have a rhyme and reason and create an image of our soul's inclination. An inclination that whenever we follow, we arrive at the source of well-being and creative power.

Our will to express our loves is a sacred thread that leads to the very core of our existence.

I have meandered off now and again, but I was always irrevocably drawn back to a few core loves. It seems almost predetermined, an illusion of choice. I couldn't help but love what I loved. Each decade the love hasn't really changed. It has only become deeper and more enriched by life's experience. Even the dark times I can now see were purposeful. They gave me strength, wit, and courage to be with and express the loves of my life.

We were born to love.
What we love and our life's journey is the bringing to earth the heaven that we love.

When my mind loses its thread to the heart, I leave love's path. I fall into the hole created by loves absence and become lost to myself. It is then that I become haunted by a mirage that has been created by humanities lost souls, a feeling of unworthiness. It whispers 'something is missing', something needs to be got or done before I can be happy, before I can be myself.

But these threads of thought are unfaithful to our heart's belief of life. They are an illusion, an apparition created by a culture of greed that has been born from all the heartless acts through the thousands of years.

These inconsolable journeys to have 'more' have pulled a veil over the heart. They have broken the trust that we are OK. That we do not need 'more' of what we do not have to be at peace. They have made the heart's beauty and power seem a foreign land, an untouchable dream reserved only for the devout or the foolish.

But now and again, through chance, trial or error, I rediscover the hearts power, and grace. I can find myself within a moment of time, free of the persuasion of what should or should not be. My expectations become dissolved in the flow of life and I allow what is, to be simply what is. In this aura of self-trust, the ghosts loosen their hold on my mind. I slip into the realms of my heart, where I become again lucid in my beloved song.

It is from this treasured chamber of ourselves that a different perception of life appears. We become embraced by hope and its compassion allows us to forgive ourself. Only then, is the unquenchable thirst to be who we are not, becomes satiated.

When we dance to tunes that are not true to our heart, the dance has little grace.

There once was a woman who enjoyed dancing. When she was young, she danced for others. When she got older, she danced for herself, and when she got wise, she danced for love.

When we act outside of the heart of us, when we do what we do without love, there is little power and no grace. But when our movement is in response to some heart's passion, some inspiration of the moment, we dance within the spirit of ourself. Our movements then become an expression of love, and we become joined by a Creation that is already in love.

A THOUGHT OF THE CHAPTER

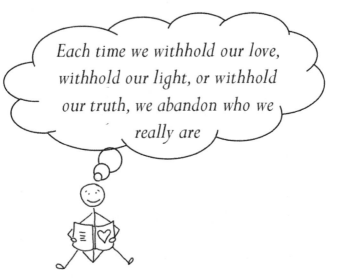

Each time we withhold our love, withhold our light, or withhold our truth, we abandon who we really are

Participation 1. *It is our heart that carries the truest care for ourselves and the greatest vision of who we love to be. The following exercise is to get to know your heart and its love.*

Exercise: Build a picture from your favourite people, things and places, things that warm your heart. it may be objects in your home that hold dear value. Songs you love. Places that have loving meanings for you. Sayings that move you. People that inspire you. Activities that ignite your fire. Colours that stir your spirit. Aspects of nature that give comfort to you. Or anything specific to you.

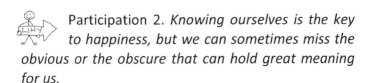

Participation 2. *Knowing ourselves is the key to happiness, but we can sometimes miss the obvious or the obscure that can hold great meaning for us.*

Exercise: Ask four friends to name three things that they know you love, that you have always had a passion about. Or qualities that you have that inspire them.

Participation 3. *What we love is not arbitrary, the things we love to do and experience are signposts of our heart's wish in life. The following exercise is to 'track' and 'trace' the loves that have moved our life, that have given it freedom and joy.*

Exercise: Examine the journey of your life, and look for the things that have always evoked your love. Look for the patterns and the deeper, unifying meaning of them.

'Take a piece of A4 paper. Turn it on its side (landscape). Draw a line along the middle of the paper; write 0 (signifying birth) at the left end of this line; write your current age at the other. Then divide this timeline into decades. In each time section, make notes of what caused passion and purpose in your life.

Participation 4. *Looking after yourself is not selfish; it's paramount. And being creative is a great way to liberate the hearts wellbeing.*

The following exercise is to know yourself, what makes you happy, what brings peace and what generates your creativity.

Exercise: Name three activities that ignite your creativity.

1.

2.

3.

Participation 5. *To be ourselves, to be true to what we hold of value is a courageous thing. But hiding our light in a hard world can be easy to do, even habitual. This exercise is to re-decide where you will be true to yourself.*

Exercise: Make a list. On it name the people or places from which you either withhold your truth, withhold your light or withhold your love.

Some people or places you may feel are necessary, perhaps at work, but others may need reconsidering, re-decide where and when you will be you.

_____
_____
_____
_____
_____
_____
_____
_____
_____
_____
_____

BEING HUMAN

Being a human is a phenomenal thing. We have a profound ability to create and give meaning to life; to discern our future, and to direct our consciousness to anything we choose.

I do want to feel that 'I am OK' so that I do not have to measure and compare who I am, what I am doing and what may be.

The struggle to be Ok with life and with ourselves has been a part of humanities story for hundreds of years. This innate human condition has been brought about by the gift of consciousness, the challenge to name the day and name who we are.

The mind's wit to compare, measure, and calculate is for our exploration of the world and for the creation of our heart's path.

But this great awareness of ourselves has its consequences, we may distinguish ourselves as separate from other people and the earth. We can step out of the truth and assume that a tree, river, bird or another person is lesser or greater than who we are.

We are given free rein to be anything we want. To challenge and change who we are, to make up our mind and by our will, make our way. We are able to explore what we do not know; to guess and take a chance in life. But this human adventuring means we do get lost, confused, feel uncertain, have doubts, get frustrated, upset and, at times, disheartened at life's struggle.

Is this being human all a mistake? Should I not be perfect, happy all the time; expressing my life with no doubt or fear. With no worry or inhibition, and certainly no anguish or boredom? Have I got it all wrong? That this part of me that is human and does err is but an illusion?

Does this humanity of us, that is bound to the gravity of earth, hold no purpose? Is this enclosure to the spirit, with all its apparent imperfections, but an error of creation; a casual slip of the hand in god's work?

Does our courage have no place, our hope no purpose? Should it be that the part of us that carries the trials of life should be rejected, admonished or simply told to go away? If we deny this humanity of ourself, we will leave a part of us behind. We will lose touch with the meaning of being a human and forfeit our time on earth.

This me of me that does not shine cannot be treated with contempt. That will break a sacred vow of life and separate myself from myself. I will become but a shadow of my soul's purpose, a fragile image of perfection with no earth beneath my feet and no heart in my voice. This is not the way, it cannot be, for whatever the parts of me that do err, and there are many, they are a part of *me*.

We are born into a moment of time, exposed to the force of life, into a place where there is no feeling we cannot have, no attitude we cannot muster if we choose it to be so. Where every thought and breath is blessed by the purpose we choose it to be.

This human life traverses the mundane and the subline. Its scope of life is astonishing. We can experience both heaven and hell in a day. We can fall in love, challenge our self with adventure and share our deepest feelings with another.To top this extraordinary experience off, being human is a self-creating experience. We alone choose our path and we alone decide its meaning. We are not a rock or a tree, fixed to a single meaning of life. We create our own gravity of purpose. To which we attempt to hold fast in the chaotic winds of life.

This wild human journey has its moments...

In life's journey, shit happens! Sometimes it's a gentle learning, sometimes it's a hard learning and sometimes it's a terrible learning.

Life has inevitable times of change, sometimes deep change...*I found myself in the supermarket with tears rolling down my face.*

The realization that I was alone had finally sunk in. I had separated from my wife of 30 years and from my kids. I was in a town where I knew no one, and I was shopping for one. All the strengths I thought I was were no longer there, and each day was a terrible emptiness.

Sometimes in life, our experience can extinguish the very grasp on who we thought we were. We can find ourselves alone, in the dark, crawling on the broken shards of all that we thought we were.

In these times, we are driven into the core of ourselves, to find the will to raise our self in the face of what seems an impossible weight. Although we do not feel it at the time, those heroic moments as we create our self-anew; the courage, purpose and dedication we summon, touches the very heart of life. Although it is a lesson we would not wish on anyone else, it does leaves us with a profound gift. In our endeavour to heal the pain we craft a beautiful gem that is without compare.

It is not the pain of life that defines us.
It is our healing of the pain that creates us.

If I look back to what has brought me to where I am now, it was certainly not what I expected. It's been an incredible journey of both calamity and beauty; of heart-wrenching - and heart-filling - experience. It has brought a staggering kaleidoscope of feelings to every year of life. It has been a personal experience, a very human experience that is held in a very human heart.

Our journey in life has gathered a unique human experience; a thousand, thousand lights have been formed from the people we have met, and the passions we have shared; the places we have been and the feeling we have felt; the loves we have given and the love we have received and of course, the trials we have endured. It is a preciousness that our heart has gathered in our journey on earth.

When our love shines through the gems of our
experience, it refracts the source of life; and
becomes our unique image of creation.

These gems of experience, that have been created in places of light and in times of darkness, are our inimitable light of life. They are the deeper meanings of ourselves, for they are what we came here for and what we will take with us when we go.

A THOUGHT OF THE CHAPTER

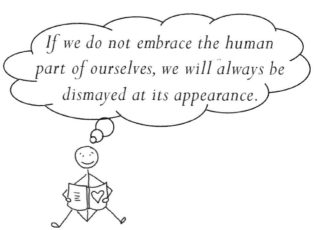

If we do not embrace the human part of ourselves, we will always be dismayed at its appearance.

Participation 1. *It is often, only after the tough events in life, after we have faced a hard learning, that we can see the benefits they gave us. Some value that we could not have got without them. The following exercise offers the chance to change the feeling, and so, the meaning we get from our past events.*

Exercise: Re-examine a time of hard learning in your life by writing down the beneficial qualities that have been born in you from it. It may be a learning, a strength, the letting go of something that no longer served you, the moving onto something that gave you greater freedom or even that you came away feeling greater self-worth for having survived it.

_____

_____

_____

_____

_____

_____

_____

_____

_____

_____

Participation 2. *The people we choose to share our life with influence much of who we will and will not be. They are our touchstones that form much of our sense of humanity.*

Exercise: Write down the names of the three people with whom you experienced the greatest trust and humanity. These will be people that are slow to judge you, allow your vulnerability and encourage the truth of you.

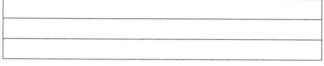

 Participation 3. *The human qualities of kindness, compassion, care, willingness to give time for another, forgiveness, integrity of word and other qualities make us human. Without them there would be a world without soul.*

The following exercises are a reflection and celebration on the value of humanity in others and yourself. It asks the question: What makes you human? What qualities does that have? What experiences give you a sense of the humanity of the world and of yourself?

Exercise: Write down your key value for humanity in others and the humanity you offer yourself. This may be recollection of experiences, a set of words or a journal of your feelings about it.

_____
_____
_____
_____
_____
_____
_____
_____
_____
_____
_____
_____
_____
_____
_____
_____
_____
_____

Participation 4. *There are some things that we will always do, that we will always be. Things that represent a value of life that is part of the core of who we are. It may show itself in kindness, or integrity or willingness. It may be any of the thousand other qualities that make up our human story.*

This exercise is to name and celebrate the humanity that you hold. (If it is not obvious, ask the people who know you, they will know what it is, what they value and trust in you.)

Exercise: What are the human equalities you hold to in life? (It will be what gives you strength, peace and a sense of freedom)

_____

_____

_____

_____

_____

_____

_____

_____

_____

_____

_____

F E A R

We have always loved;
fear is something we have learnt.

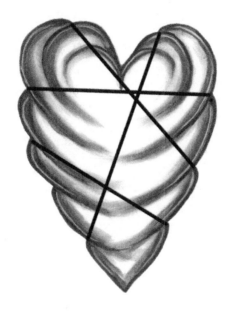

I long to walk fearlessly through life. To tread the unknown without trepidation, without dis-ease of movement or thought. So, every step carries the whole of me, has the power to touch the heart of the earth and be a celebration of the power of life.

We can't let go of what we cannot see, and we can't heal what we cannot feel.

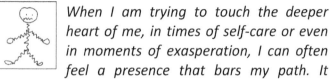 *When I am trying to touch the deeper heart of me, in times of self-care or even in moments of exasperation, I can often feel a presence that bars my path. It makes me feel uncertain, often unworthy, and always alone. It is made from the anxiety and stress of life and is known by the name of 'Fear'. It is not necessarily a specific fear that I can name. It's more of an entity, made from the accumulated pain of life, ghosts in the subconscious mind that cause the hundred little apprehensions in a day.*

The fears that we carry do no honour to our hearts purpose. they close the door to its light and make us deaf to its wisdom.

This is a tough chapter; it is about fear and nobody likes talking about it, it makes us feel… fearful. But as the presence of fear erodes our love, it needs to be known it if we are ever to have a chance in love.

If we do not recognise the presence of fear, we will unknowingly accept it as a companion.

I was sitting in a café writing and fighting the noise of drilling as workmen dug up the road outside. After a while, it became less of a distraction and after an hour, I hardly noticed it. Two hours later it suddenly stopped and the air became at peace. I then felt the relief in my body and my mind became at ease.

It was then that I realized how much I had unconsciously suffered by its noise.

If I measure the fear that I carry by the absence of the love that I feel, the weight of my fears becomes apparent. This is a dreadful awareness to have because it shows how accustomed I have become to the fears I hold.

When we respond to our fears, we take advice from something that does not care for our happiness.

Fear is insipid. It creeps in through holes within our integrity. The lesions created from the doubt and uncertainty we have of ourselves, and of life. Fear and its siblings, anxiety and stress, are terrible companions on this journey. They do not have fun and they do not seek joy. They take us out of the precious moment of the now into what was or what may or may not be. They create the illusion of a purpose outside of the heart of ourself. So, we unknowingly abandon the sanctuary of the heart, and send our mind on impossible journeys; to search for security in the world outside of ourself, in other people and things.

The trouble with fear is that it is the opposite of love. It closes the heart and drives out the light. In fear, we do not give but we always do in love. We do not have hope in fear but we do in love. One gives courage, one does not. One peace, one not.

We attract what we love in the same way as we attract what we fear.

Love and fear are the two primordial powers of attraction and action. We are constantly trying to move towards what we love, and away from what we fear.

When I am in love I do care for the world and myself, but when I am in fear, my ability to care becomes broken by a wish to win and not lose. A selfishness that has little care for others and no real care for myself.

I watch the 'why I do what I do', to see if it comes from love or fear. Whenever I am being caused to travel the darker paths, my job is to do the things that can shift the balance of power, to sway the mind into a more benign view of ourself and the world.

It is the return-to-self that happens when we let go
of fear, that allows us to remember
who we love to be.

We can't take fear on this journey into the unknown;
it will only attract the ghosts of our yesterdays

If we do not have some love in who we are and what
we do, we will make room for fear. We will step back
from the inspired action in fear of the unknown. We
will hold onto our truth in fear of what others may
think. We will get in the way of the light and create a
shadow of ourself. We then, over time, assume that
the shadow is who we are and accept it as a true
companion. But this is not so, fear is an illusion. It
evaporates whenever we touch what is truly
important.

Tread lightly in life, fear not what may or may
not happen, for you will still be you and you are
OK, you are enough. Nothing, not even death,
can take that away from you.

A THOUGHT OF THE CHAPTER

You cannot love in fear and you will not fear in love.

Participation 1. *When we name what it is that we fear, we have a chance to reclaim our power and decide again who we wish to be.*

Exercise: Write down the list of your fears, silly ones, and big ones, recognise them and then burn the list. (a few to consider are listed below)

Fear of failure/success

Fear of what other people think or do not think of you

Fear of not having enough money

Fear of not having enough time

Fear of losing one's job or partner

Fear of yesterday, the consequences of what we did or did not do

Fear of tomorrow, what may or may not happen

Fear of God

Fear of illness

Fear of getting old

Fear of death

Fear of not being enough

Fear of not being able to cope with whatever happens tomorrow, next week, next year.

Participation 2. *Letting go of things that do not serve you is always a good practice. This exercise is an ongoing practice to just relax.*

Exercise: Take time during the day to recognise the tension, stress, anxiety or fear that has accumulated, and the harm it is doing to your well-being. Then invite hope; relax, breathe ... bid the fear farewell.

PAUSE ...

Hi! Thank you for your company on this journey so far. We have reached just over halfway through the story. Before we continue into the last chapters, I thought it would be good to do a recap. To go over what has been covered and why we have been there.

We began with the story of how this journey came about. We then looked at the Mind and its inevitable influence on our wellbeing. How its preoccupation is driven by the power of our feelings and the force of habit. How it, of itself, is just a servant that can only serve according to the training that it is given.

We then touched on Will and its self-creating ability, a power that is created by the reason *why* we do what we do. We then acknowledged that our will is sacrosanct, that it will either confirm or dissipate our integrity.

We then travelled into Memory. How its constant presence separates us from the power of the now. This, in turn, makes us unwilling and unable to step into the great adventure of the unknown. The place that holds our greater self and our future.

Then we spent some time in the Heart, the source of so many wonders of the world. And visioned its power and its purpose. And then the big question of how can we know our own heart.

Then we met fear, loves opposing force. And how its presence will always put out the fire of the heart.

We are now coming up to the last few chapters of this work and I thought it would be good to ask you, the reader, a question. *Why bother to do this work with self?*

I have asked myself this often when the weather of my journey is tough. And some of the work so far has been tough. In clement times, it is easy to find a pretty answer, but in rough times, they are hard to find. But when it is found, it is always the great unvarnished truth.

This naked truth is always good, it has power without distraction. And we need that power, because this path is not for the faint-hearted. It calls for self-accountability and an openness to ourselves, the all of us. And because of that, to life itself. It is a journey of becoming conscious, a journey that has no final destination.

Participation 1. *If there was a god that could grant what we wish, they would have trouble knowing what we really wanted. We issue such a cacophony of wants, wishes and desires in a day, that they would not easily discern our true wish of life.*

The why we do what we do gives us power. So, the question is - Why bother? Why make the effort in the journey of self-awareness and self-discovery? What is your purpose and how well does it stir your heart, for without the power of purpose we will not see the way.

133

Exercise: Write words or draw an image that captures your sense of purpose in your journey of self-discovery.

_____
_____
_____
_____
_____
_____
_____
_____
_____
_____
_____
_____
_____
_____
_____
_____
_____
_____
_____
_____
_____

As I have asked you, the reader. It is only fair that I give you, my reason. I bother because it is the only way that I maybe truly happy. The only way to liberate the love that is held in the heart. I do this work because, on this journey of consciousness, the paths that take me to desolate places become less. The strengths to become whole again after turmoil are easier to summon. Judgements of other people and myself become less and my relationships to other people become richer.

I hold less onto yesterday's pain and forgive often, especially myself.

The bottom line is that I love more and fear less.

So, the adventure continues...toward becoming whole, toward love and the sacredness of self.

VULNERABILITY & FRAGILITY

Vulnerability and fragility, do not confuse the two. One lives in fear, the other in love, and it is only love that can dissolve the illusion of fear.

When I was young, I was happy in my state of vulnerability. Open to life, I explored its mystery with wonder. But life can be tough, and people not always kind. So, in the times of unhappiness or pain, a part of me was built that fears it can be hurt or broken - a fragile self.

This fragile self will raise its head when we feel threatened or unworthy. Its presence makes us reluctant to expose our vulnerability, our honest self to others, for fear of getting hurt, for fear of seeming weak and for fear of what they may see of us. So, we put on a face that is not our whole truth, only the truth we think acceptable.

This fragile self plays havoc with my attempt to know the heart. It not only hides my truth from others, it hides my truth from me. It denies me the ability to trust myself, to allow me to be me. But as my journey deepens, I have recognised, more often than not, my feelings of fragility as a signpost, a warning of my immanent inhumane attitude to myself or others. I see the walls my fragile self has created. So, I soften, cease my derision, and call upon the vulnerability of me to reappear.

I ask myself to trust again the benevolence of life and the benevolence of me. When I can do this, I look back on my fragile self and the fears that it carries, and it seems such a silly thing to do, to huff and puff at life. But no doubt I will do it again, probably within the hour, and fall back into the illusion of fear and assume that I am unworthy to be me.

138

The vulnerability within us carries an innocence that has no thoughts of how things should or should not be, only a wonder that life is.

 When I can accept my vulnerability as the truth of me, I no longer have to be something for others. I know that who I am is already something.

It is easy to think of our vulnerability as weak, it lacks the power of deception. Our emotions are exposed for all to read like an open book. Although we do need a bit of buff and pretence to get by in life, we always need to know our truth, especially for ourselves. In accepting our vulnerability, we do feel our truth. It may not always be pretty, but it is honest. It is who we are at the time, without pretence or deception. And that is always powerful!

The fragility we feel, because of the fears that we carry, causes us to hardly ever touch the moment of the now, because our fragility is too busy telling it how it should be.

When we allow our vulnerable self, we cease the war that the fragile self-perpetuates. We settle into ourselves and become our own friend. And if we step deeper into the vulnerability, accept it as a gift to ourself of ourself, we meet the true self, a self that is awake to the moments of life. It is then that we can know our own heart.

It is from this place that the secrets I battled to find in my fragile self reveal themselves, and the view can be breath-taking. I feel the greater truth of who I am. I am a part of all that I see; no lesser or greater than a flower or a tree, another person, or a God.

When we accept our vulnerability, we heal our lost self and reunite the family of ourselves. We know, again, that we need nothing more to be who we are; that who we are is OK, is enough. And that knowing is everything because it is the deeper truth of ourselves.

As I try to hold onto the gentleness of this vulnerable self, the fragile self is never far away, whispering in my ear 'this innocence should not be exposed', 'take up the hard mantel of care-less intention again'. It so wants me to be the strengths that make me weak unto myself, strengths that have no care for the soul of me. It will say that I am unworthy, not strong enough, not bright enough, not wise enough to accept this vulnerability as a truth of myself. But this is the illusion of fear because within my vulnerability there is an indomitable strength, an unconquerable spirit that is the truth of me.

When we love ourselves, the all of us, the good, bad, and the ugly, we have created compassion and that compassion will then extends to all that we see.

A THOUGHT OF THE CHAPTER

To be open and vulnerable to ourselves is not always comfortable, but it is always our truth.

Participation 1. *Our sense of fragility closes the heart and our sense of vulnerability is in an open heart. These two qualities of vulnerability and fragility can seem the same, but one is rooted in love, the other fear.*

Exercise: Create a mind map of associated qualities and attitudes that describe the sense of fragility and vulnerability. Expand it as much as you want with the meanings of the qualities of vulnerability and fragility. Some words to consider, in no particular order, are:

Open, closed, hard, soft, to hold back, to give, honesty, guarded, kindness, hostility, isolation, inclusion, growth, to receive, friendship, trust, distrust, fear, courage, love, relaxed, tense, protection, expansion, contraction, progress, love.

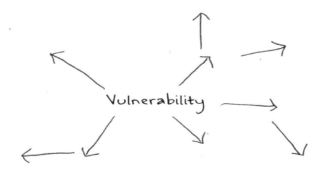

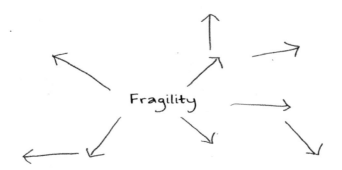

LEARNING TO LOVE YOURSELF

We can't read our heart through the turmoil of our own inhospitality. Because all its guidance and love are smudged by the defiance we hold against ourself; to the parts of us we deem unworthy or inadequate.

The true test of self-love comes not when the sun is shining, but when the storm strikes. When the strengths I thought I was, no longer keep me afloat. It is then that it becomes too easy to sink into the dark places where reside the daemons that seem to carry no wish for my happiness. They are strong and know me well. They know the open wounds because that is where they were born, and have been nurtured with every doubt I have had about myself.

Wherever we go we take ourselves with us. We are and will always be our closest companion. We know our loves, fears, hopes and dreams intimately, because we have lived within the world of our thoughts and feelings throughout our life. It is a relationship that started when we were born and has been augmented by every year of our life.

If we are not mindfull in our self care, its all too easy for our relationship with ourselves to become a lost cause, something that we just have to put up with. This was how my relationship with myself seemed a few years ago. It was like a broken marriage...

You no longer talk lovingly to each other, no longer go for happy walks together or share laughter about the idiosyncrasies of life. You want to keep the illusion that it's still possible, and sometimes it seems OK, but you know in your gut that it's not true; there has been too much hurt. The relationship is broken and it's been broken for a long time. You've papered over the cracks with reluctant patience, but it's just not working. The trouble is you can't escape; you're stuck in an unloving relationship.

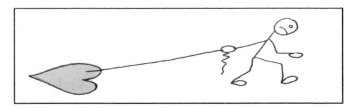

So, you accept the pain, become used to the atmosphere of slight belligerence and hostility that seems to arise for no reason and get on trying to live your life as best you can. It's their fault, of course, they just don't care anymore! And they are too good at poking the bits that hurt most. So, you avoid them whenever possible, even try to pretend they do not exist. As long as you keep yourself 'busy', this does work for a while, but when the busy stops it's then that you feel a distress, a loneliness, and a sadness that you just cannot understand. It's as if something, someone is missing from your life. So, you become busy again, an addict of stuff in an attempt to fill the void that this 'missing' causes. Eat, drink and try to be merry for tomorrow is another day and perhaps it will be better…

Of all the relationships in life, the relationship with ourselves is the most important.

Our relationship with ourselves affects so much of how life happens and how we are within it.

It determines how much we nurture our love, and how well we manage the difficult times. And of course, it affects deeply everyone we share life with. Yet it remains for many of us, a struggle; a puzzle with no picture to work from.

I do find this strange... You would have thought that after the thousands of years of human endeavour, and the millions of writings created by the great sages of history; that a loving peace and happiness with ourselves would be simple. That the paths would be laid out, signposted and easy to follow. Where each generation would find it easier because of the work already accomplished. But this does not seem to be so. It is as if each person has to create for themselves, the peace of their life. And where each generation has to make their love anew.

I was sitting in a café, working on this chapter, and asked a group of middle-aged women, who were at the next table, their thoughts about it. I explained to them that I was working on a book about self-love and asked for their comments about learning to love yourself. After their initial shock, embarrassment, and giggles, that this unspoken subject should be spoken of openly. There were the comments, 'that would take years' and 'I would need psychoanalysis for that'.

Their response was not surprising, loving ourself is no easy matter. Perhaps even more now, there is so much that distracts the mind; entices us into adventures outside of our heart. Just too many illusions of love created by the commercial world that erode our wellbeing, and so break the will that cares for our self.

The measure of our self-love is in the courage we have to embrace the parts of us that act as if we do not care.

A story: there once lived a mirror that sat on the wall in a family house. It was quite a nice spot to be, for it saw the family often as they went out and came home. The children were particularly fun as they would look at the mirror and pull lots of funny faces, and the mirror loved to show them their bright happy eyes. The mother would look into the mirror on her way out to check that she was looking good and sometimes, look into her eyes and smile. But most people did not have time for this, they hid this gift of the mirror from themselves behind their 'I'm too busy to say hello' face and turned away before the mirror could give it to them. This was especially true of the father, he never had time to see himself.

The mirror suspected that he did not really want to see himself, because in the small glances he did take, the mirror saw the struggle and pain he was carrying in life and the hurt he was doing to himself because of it. But one day the father did stop and look; for some reason, he did not rush off but just looked.

At first, all he saw was his hard, busy face, but after a while, that seemed to fade. He began to see the anguish that the struggles of life that had put there, the lines of his age, his tired eyes, and the sadness they carried. The mirror felt the man's wish to look away, but urged him to keep looking, to see beyond the pain that he saw, to see the star he held deep within his eyes.

Suddenly, it seemed that time stopped and all that was in the world was the father and the mirror.

The mirror then performed its true function and gave the man the whole truth of himself, the picture of his struggles, and also his beautiful gentle soul.

Tears began to form in the eyes of the father and he spoke these words. 'I love you; I am sorry for the pain that you carry, please forgive me and thank you for being there and carrying my life'.

It's easy to love yourself when you feel good, tricky when you feel bad, and seemingly impossible when you're feeling ugly.

I do not love the grumpy of me, the sad of me, the hostile of myself, the parts of me that act as if I do not care. I name them as 'not me' and so drive a sword into myself, separating consciousness into the good and the bad, the worthy and the unworthy. I declare this part of me a disturber of the peace a foe to my purpose, an antagonist to my harmony and so become the intolerant parent to the hurting child within; the part of me that is in distress, in need of understanding, in need of love.

Self-love is self-care.

A few years ago, in a period of tough learning, I happened to see my face in the mirror and saw a ghost. That ghost was me! It was a shadow of who I thought I was. Within the eyes was a desolate self. A desperate, pained self that was carrying the accumulated struggles of my life. I was shocked and so sad that I should have done this to myself. I felt both frightened by it and ashamed of it. This was me.

A part of me that every time it had cried out for attention, to be recognised, to be loved, to be healed, I had shunned it, told it that it was not who I was, and locked this hurting child of myself in a dark room, away from the light of my consciousness. Away from its guardian, its parent, me!

I had always been pretty good at being honest to myself, but this image of me begged for a deeper level of self-acceptance and forgiveness. It called for a supreme act of will that I felt unable to muster. And to be honest, I'm not sure that I really wanted to. It seemed such a terrible journey to do. Surely, it would be easier just to close my eyes to its grief. But that could never bring real happiness, only build an illusion of self. And I needed the truth of me, the whole me, if I was ever to have the power to be true to my heart.

Talk gently to yourself about what you truly care for, so you will know who you really are.

I had often talked *at* myself in dismay, "WTF!" In a rant, "you %@#!..." or in the way of insistence, "you better do this or...." but rarely did I talk to myself, as a friend, a companion.

Talk to myself in a way that made me feel that I truly cared for myself, cared that I was loved.

To be loved by another is wonderful, to be loved by yourself is freedom.

We are not one thing; we are a family unto ourselves with all the idiosyncrasies and depths of relationships that families have. And the parent to this family is our consciousness; our point of awareness, action and decision. It is from this place we talk to the family of ourselves. And how we talk will determine what kind of relationship we have with ourselves.

The power to love ourselves comes from our heart. It holds an infinite resource of love that will never fail us, because the heart's purpose is love. It's what it does.

When I am in the loved part of me, I accept the unloved parts of myself. So, it is to the unloved that I need to bring the light that is held by the loved.

When you love someone, you care for their love of life, their well-being and their happiness. You wish the best for them, accept them as they are. And when they are in difficulty, you give them your patience and support. Like a mother's love for her child, it is steadfast and unconditional.

A THOUGHT OF THE CHAPTER

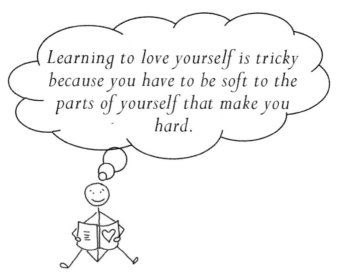

Learning to love yourself is tricky because you have to be soft to the parts of yourself that make you hard.

Participation - Learning to Love Yourself

Participation 1. *We often talk at ourselves, but don't often talk to ourselves; as a friend, as a companion. In a way that accepts the good, bad and ugly as the family of ourselves.*

Exercise: Talk to yourself in the mirror. Be nice ☺ Even looking in your eyes, smiling, and saying hello is good.

Participation 2. *There are always parts of us that are loveable. Sometimes we need to be reminded what they are. Some may be silly, but loveable, others may be more seriously lovable. Choose one [or some] that brings an inner smile to yourself. To get a broader truth of this, you may also wish to ask people you know what they think makes you lovable.*

Exercise: Complete the following: I love myself because...

_____

_____

_____

_____

_____

_____

_____

_____

L O V E

Pure love is a white light that by our endeavour, refracts into a thousand colours.

The heart knows what the mind cannot see and the soul lives in what the heart loves.

 It is our heart that knows love and it will always be our heat that we go if we wish to be in its company. Of all the powers we have, our love is the greatest. When we give love to life, it always gives us more in return. It dispels fear, powers our will and gives us the courage to step into the unknown.

I love many things, the sea, the smell of a rose, a wooded glade in autumn, the sound of the laughter of a child, and so many more. I can think of reasons why I love what I love, but the loves I feel are greater than the reasons my mind can construct about them.

The mind can create a picture, but it is our love that gives it colour and depth.

Love is what we find beautiful; a feeling of communion with something that the mind does not fully understand. But when we are in our love, it does make total sense.

Our loves beckon us forward. They carry an inherent trust that gives us courage to be more than who we were. And when we are in love, the mind is released from the catacombs of its memory. It is able to travel beyond the confines of its education, to see what the heart already knows.

Everyone has their own unique picture of love. Passions that entice them to participate in life.

Some people really love cats, some to tango and some love the dawn.
Some love to listen to jazz, some to walk the dog and some to collect stamps.
Some love pottery, some football, and some love trains.
Some love to cook, some to dance and some love to play charades.
Some love lions, some to ride horses and some love to dance in the rain.
Some love coffee, some the theatre, and some love shoes.
Some love trees, some to party, and some love to make people smile.
Some love to play the piano, some love cars, and some love the autumn.
Some people love chess, some hats, and some just love.

There is, consistently and irrevocably, a stream of love issuing from this earth, and it is made by the heart of us. It is an eclectic love but it is love and when we love, life lives.

When we share what we love with a kindred spirit, more than who we are happens. The heavens open and a thousand lights rain upon us.

Love is the source of all heroic deeds and all the lights of the world, for all great achievements are born from an idea of love. Without love, hope has no home, courage no direction, and fortitude no purpose.

It is why we dance and why we give. It brings meaning to life for without love there is no colour, no passion, and no joy. Its presence can sustain us through the darkest hours, the wildest storms and can give comfort in the loneliest of times. It calms the troubled mind, mends the broken heart, and brings home the wandering soul. It is a bond that can bring a nation together, a family together and its presence holds our self together. It gives strength for a leap of faith, a trust in life, a wish for tomorrow and a living of the day.

Love is why we live.

While I was sitting within a grove of trees, my gaze came to rest upon a single tree. I tried to see this tree as it was, to feel its life without my conditions of how I thought it should be. So, I waited for another way to understand this tree, resisting the distractions in me that so wanted to tell the tree what it was. I waited for the tree to tell *me* who *it* was. Ever so slowly, an awareness of the tree grew in me of its life, its interconnectivity to the other trees, the air, and the earth. This tree felt singular in its purpose; not a different type of tree or a daffodil, but the tree that it was.

It felt like it had no doubt of *what* it was or *why* it was. The power of the tree's self-identity was total. It was *in love with* being the tree that it was.

This irrevocable love that is evident in nature, feels so different from the human experience of love. Ours seems a kaleidoscopic chaotic love affair. Unfixed to the singular love that a tree has, it is a helter-skelter ride of highs and lows, where our everchanging will causes it to come and go all too easily.

The tree does not have to make it, it is in it! We have to summon it; create its opportunities and beckon it into our lives. And we do this each day; rekindle the sparks of our purpose to find again our love. Because we do long to be in love in what we do, with another and with who we are. We love to love, love to share, love to give, love to make things that shine, and of course, we love to be happy.

It seems that the human task is to 'make love', to give birth to it by our will. And this we do, in our choices of passion and in the struggles we endure to bring our heart's love to life.

This gift of sanctuary that is love is obvious in the eyes of a child, they love easily. When we were young the first snow is awesome, a sandpit a world of adventure. We fell in love with the rain, puddles; the simplest of things.

This natural response of love faded as we grew up, put aside by the expediency of life and the demands of the world. But it is never lost, the wish to love is always within us, urging us to recreate again the love we once knew, to find again what it is that our heart already knows.

To love is in our very nature; we become a distraught apparition of life without its presence. But when we love the heavens open.

And the deeper we love the deeper the peace. There is no end to the depths that can be sought. There is no limitation to what may be when we love.

I do love to dance within the music of love. She leads with a potent touch of cherishment. She nourishes the soul and sets fire to the spirit. When I am with her the noise of time stops and the beauty of the world unfurls. It feels as if the only purpose of life is to embrace love, to be with this essence of light. But in time, life will make the music falter. I will lose the rhythm and fall out of love. The memory of its beauty will fade, and the truth that it is all that is important will become again, for a while, a forgotten dream, until I hear her music again and fall back into love.

When we let go of our love, we become the ghost of our self, lamenting the absence of the very thing that we have abandoned, love. We become stranded, like a beached whale, lost from the life that loves presence brings. The mind then renews its troubled search to fill the hole of love's absence. Of course, the heart will wait patiently for me as my mind struggles in this errant task until, by chance or reason, I bring her close again; recreate the music and make love again.

When we make love, we enter the flow of life and rebuild our communion with its source.

I was in Timbavati, a nature reserve for the sacred white lions of Africa. The reserve was run by a woman who had deep experience and love of the white lions. I was with a group of people on a shamanic retreat, led by a woman who had profound abilities in reading the forces of nature. It was during this time that I understood another aspect of love; the love of a soul purpose.

I witnessed these two powerful women in a challenging dialogue. One was like a lioness, with her great prowess and courage, the other, the woodland deer, alert, listening with its infinite patience and trust.

They were each magnificent, unique in the power of the love they felt of life. Their authority and power did not stem from ambition; nor from any self-esteem.

It emanated from the dedication to their souls' calling. They were both beautiful, each were in love with who they were and why they were.

A THOUGHT OF THE CHAPTER

Be not timid with your love for no great life ever happened without it.

Participation 1. *A picture is worth a thousand words. We can learn a lot about our love from the deeper image that our mind holds of love.*

The following exercise is to evoke the minds metaphor of love and is a celebration of the importance of love.

Exercise: Think about the way your mind loves. Ask yourself what metaphor would best characterise this this state.

When I am in love with what I am doing, it's like what?

_____

_____

_____

_____

_____

_____

_____

_____

_____

_____

_____

To further explore this metaphor, ask yourself.

Is there anything else about [whatever metaphor you came up with]?

_____

_____

_____

_____

_____

_____

_____

_____

And finally ask yourself

Does it have a color, shape, location in or around you?

_____

_____

_____

_____

_____

_____

_____

_____

_____

Knowing our loves is not only an inspiration, it is also a great way to get 'happier'. The following exercise is to bring to the forefront of your mind the things that cause you to love, and the feelings that arise in you when love happens.

Exercise: *Take some time to celebrate love.* Write down four things that evoke your sense of love. What people, environments or activities have you found allow your sense of love to arise, and the feeling you have because of them?

_____

_____

_____

_____

_____

_____

_____

_____

And three things that cause you to fall out of love. What people, environments or activities cause your sense of love to expire? (Some may be necessary in your life, some may not.)

_____

_____

_____

_____

_____

_____

Participation 2. Remember your love. *Our time is precious, but life is a busy place where we can forget to do the things that we know bring love into our loves.*

Exercise: What loves have you put aside because you felt you had no time? They don't have to be big things, they can just be lovely, silly things.

_____

_____

_____

_____

_____

_____

_____

_____

_____

FORGIVENESS

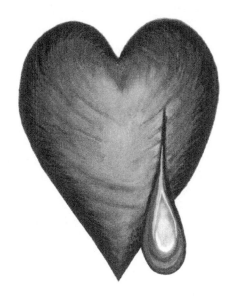

Each time I blame other people for how I am feeling, I relinquish my authority.

Each time I blame myself for who I am being, I fracture my consciousness, separating myself into the worthy and the unworthy, the loved me and the unloved.

Forgiving others about what they did or did not do is not really about them, it's about letting go of the pain we hold because of it. But this chapter is really about the forgiveness we have for ourselves. Giving ourselves freedom from the pain we carry because of ourselves.

Life is messy and I am really not perfect. And it is not fair of me to think that I could be. So, I do not need to forgive myself for being stupid, stupid is part of living, so there is nothing to forgive. But I can forgive myself for feeling inadequate, for feeling that I am not enough. Because these are the parts of me that need to know I care, that need to know I will not leave them alone and without light.

At the end of a weekend retreat, I was in a deep connection to the heart. It radiated a kindness and benevolence that was most loving. I found myself experiencing a powerful sense of self-forgiveness, a healing for the unforgiven parts of me that I carried.

A few days later, after the great forgiveness had subsided, and I had returned to my normal level of self-attitude.

I compared the feelings I had in myself, to the deep sense of mercy that I had experienced at the retreat. I realized, by the absence of the self-love I had experienced at the retreat, that I have gone about in life being unforgiving to myself. An intolerance that I unknowingly carried.

This was alarming; comparing the loving freedom I had felt from my forgiveness and the hurt I did to myself by its absence.

I know there is a part of me that I have hurt. I have not always been easy on myself. It wasn't a conscious act, but more often just a background impatience; and at times hostility to parts of myself that I just didn't understand. This trail of injustice, hidden deep within my memories of life, has left its mark upon me. And in my times of peace and reconciliation, I have felt its sorrows, its tears and its pain.

This wound will not go away; it is part of the story that has made me who I am. I am, after all, the all of me. There is nothing that happens in me that is not me. It seems obvious as I write this, but when I really know it, I cease to dismember myself with blame or derision. I become the tolerant parent to the all of me.

I will remember to remember to forgive myself often. Because I see that the walls I have crafted from fear and indifference to myself make me seem alone and without light.

Each day we start again, try with our heart to be the person we love to be. We never stop, never do less than our best, it may be a misinformed best or even a grumpy best, but it was always the best at the time. It's been the story of our extraordinary life. So, we should forgive ourself for any hurt we have done because of who we thought we should have been, but were not.

We can always be better, stronger, wiser, brighter, more loving; without the wish to be so we would never grow in ourselves. But when that wish turns sour, when it ceases to be the inspiration and becomes the tyrant, we cast out our love, renounce a part of ourselves with blame and so, lay waste our peace and well-being.

It is through our acts of forgiveness that we become whole unto our self, for when we embrace our self in care, we heal the rift between the lonely of us and the source of our selves. We become the mother to the family of ourselves, giving care and space, so we may grow and learn without remorse.

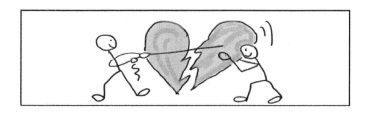

When I can I do this, I know I am the loved and the unloved. They are accepted as part of the irrevocable story of who I am. That admission dissolves the barriers to my heart. It allows me to join a part of me that is fearless and so, so loving.

This is the part of me that I wish communion with. It holds the light. For when I am there, I do see clearly; I see the way and feel the power to do it. Sadly, when I am not there, I neither see the way nor feel the power.

So, I often write messages to myself, to bring light to the dark of me, to help make conscious my life.

Forgive my impatience for I do often forget the trust you hold in me and I am often insensitive to the love you are.Forgive my attitudes and careless wanderings that cause me to let go of your touch of life. I ask that you look again at me with your eyes and bless the truth of our life that I hold within the heart of me.

As I enter this chamber of my heart, I hold myself in self-forgiveness, for every division that I carry will only reject me into the shadowlands of my yesterdays.

A THOUGHT OF THE CHAPTER

We always do our best at the time but sometimes do not forgive ourselves for not being perfect.

Participation 1. *We have thousands of thoughts and feelings each day. Some are useful, some are not. Unless we make a conscious decision of what we want to take forward in our lives, the mind will continue to rummage the days doings, into the night and the following day. This is a practice for 'letting go'. To de-clutter the mind and to help us to move forward.*

Exercise: At the end of the day, before you go to sleep, make a conscious choice to let go of the day's journey. Allow it to be what it was, the good and the bad of it. Give it gratitude and acceptance and let it be. And in the morning, as the mind reassembles itself and begins to replay yesterday's thoughts, decide again, what are useful and what are not.

Participation 2. *We exist in a 'living timeline' where yesterday's experiences live in us today, according to the feelings we have about them. These feelings can be changed at any time if we choose to think about it differently, give our experience a different meaning. The following exercise is to heal an unforgiven part of yourself that you that you now feel able to forgive, able to embrace as a part of yourself.*

Exercise: Recall one or more events in your life where you have not forgiven yourself for what happened. For what you did not do but felt should have, or for what you did do and felt you should not have done.

Choose an event that you now feel you can now forgive yourself for not being perfect. This can also be used as a daily practice.

_____

_____

_____

_____

_____

_____

_____

_____

_____

_____

_____

_____

DIVINING THE DIVINE SELF

We are never really far away from the stream of life. It's only our thought that we are that makes it so.

A few years ago, I was at a house auction looking for a new home. I had always hankered after a chapel, this time my dream got the better of me. I bought a huge dilapidated chapel and its annex.

As I stood on the gallery, looking down onto the 300 ft x120ft space below, the pulpit, the pews and all the detailed woodwork, it was awesome and frightening. There was so much to do. It had serious dry rot in many of the timbers, and into the 4ft deep walls. The rotting timbers needed to be ripped out and the walls stripped and re rendered before anything else could happen. Then a 140 ft reinforced steel joist was put in to support the new first floor. This would provide space for the three new bedrooms, bathroom, living area and art studio that would be my new home.

The pews were removed and much of its wood cleaned, oiled and used as the kitchen work tops, skirting and partitioning. The old wiring was removed and replaced, plumbing was put in for central heating, kitchen and a bathroom.

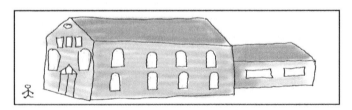

It was an immense job. I thought I could do it in a year, but in the end, it would take three. Friends thought I was mad to take it on, and looking back, it did seem a wild thing to do.

As I sat exhausted in the chaos and the dust, I was facing myself like no other time in my life, my love and my despair. There was nowhere to hide from my troubled self; the distraught and lonely part of me. A me of me that had always been there, but never really acknowledged. I could no longer escape and had to make amends to this forlorn part of me; heal the embedded sadness that I carried. It was during this time that I learned to be brave unto myself. As I converted the unloved chapel into a beautiful home, I did the same to myself. I embraced the vulnerable me. I gave it space to be and listened to its stories. We shared our dreams, our loves and our tears, as we learned to trust each other as we become one.

I had searched for years 'out there' for the meaning of life. Yet the truth is that it is we who create it. And it is we who are accountable for the meanings that our life creates. This was a sobering epiphany, but not a lonely realization.

I found the God I have been looking for so many years, and that God was me! No lesser or greater than the God of you. My commitment to self-acceptance had cleared a mist that had surrounded my life and my heart. It revealed a chamber of resilience and power within myself that would become my dearest companion.

We all carry this inner chamber within ourselves, it waits unwearyingly for our presence; for the times when we allow ourselves to be vulnerable. To be open and willing to love and accept ourselves.

Our willingness to embrace our vulnerability is equal to the trust we have in ourselves.

During the time of renovating the chapel, I went on a retreat in Wales. There were eight of us on this self-discovery course. At dawn we went to a waterfall and into its ice-cold waters, followed by ceremonies, meditations, solitude and times in nature. In the evening, we shared music created from shamanic journeying. One day, we walked up onto the moors to an ancient stone circle. Here, we spent some hours connecting to, and creating music from its ancient space. When the music finished, as I sat in silence and peace, an image and set of words both came clearly to mind. They spoke of my relationship to the core of me; to that divine part of me that I had sought to know over many years.

The words were profound and I knew that in the days and months that followed their truth would fade. So, from that day, every morning, I draw an image and write its meaning, as a way to remember what I gave to myself that day.

*I trust the chamber of myself for it has been built
with intention and care.*

There is, within me an indigenous space that has
been co created by creations love and my care of it.

*I ask that God (whatever word works for you)
fill it with its presence.*

I ask because we must always ask for that which we
seek.

I will listen for its guidance and love.

Then it is my job to listen its presence and respond.

We carry a fraction of light that life's disparate journey can never ruin. This spirit is our essence, our simple truth and its beauty is, like ourselves, incomparable.

It is a sense of purpose and an inclination of love that will never leave us. It is the light that pulls us forward, and the song that charms us into the living moment. It is the ineffable story of who we are, a life that has been nurtured by the thousand million moments of our love's purpose. It is the sacred fraction of life that is our divine nature; it is our love.

I find myself at the door to this chamber whenever I have mercy on myself. When I recognise my fallibility as an inevitable truth of life, a consequence of my innocent journey through time. I enter when I recognise my innocence as the greater truth of who I am.

This is true and beautiful but not always easy…

How can something that is so near, often seem so far? Why do we forget where love is and too often treat ourselves with disdain or indifference?

I do forget and am habitually indifferent to myself. I often struggle to see the way and easily fail to find the aptitude to take me home.

A story – There was once a tired and hungry man who had been looking for days to find somewhere to rest and eat. In the distance he saw a farm house and made his way there. He knocked on the from door and in hope of food and a place to rest.

The farmer opened the door and asked the traveller his intention. I need a place to sleep and some food please, the traveller responded. Can you pay for it? the farmer asked. No, I have no money, the traveller replied. Well, said the farmer. You can earn some money by collecting coloured balls that are hidden in the forest, then I will give you a bed and some food. For each a green, yellow, blue, red or white one that you find, I will give you 10p. And if you happen to find a silver or gold one, I will give you £10 for either of them.

So, the man set off into the woods in search of the coloured balls. Right, he thought, I will concentrate on the silver and gold balls, that will give me enough money for food and a bed. So, he searched all day for the silver and gold balls, he saw a few yellow ones, some green and a couple of red ones, but he passed them by in his search for the silver and gold. At the end of the day, he went back to the farmhouse empty handed. He was really hungry now and begged the farmer for some food. No, he said, only if you earn it. You may sleep in the barn and try again tomorrow. The next day the traveller set off into the forest again to search for the balls, but again he found no silver or gold. So, he slept in the barn again, hungry. The next day he started again, but he was desperate now, so he stopped looking for the silver and gold and just picked up any balls that he could find. By midday he had quite a collection of coloured balls. As he continued his search, he noticed a bright light within the woods, it was a silver ball! He smiled and picked it up. But he did not stop his search for the other coloured balls.

And by the end of the day, he had a great pile of coloured balls and two silver ones and one gold one. That night he was fed and slept in a warm house.

I have found silver and gold moments many times and they are heavenly. They are places of no careless thought, no mindless wandering, only a wandering in the music of providence. When I am there, there is nowhere else I wish to be, no one else I wish to be. I feel settled into the very heart of me, whole, healed, and happy.

When we can find these moments, we do feel cherished. An emotion arises, like the meeting of two old friends who have been absent from each other for far too long. A hush descends and the talking stops, and we are surrounded in the whisper of knowings. Troubles melt away, as we become part of all that we see. There is nothing to do or be, other than to love in the light of this freedom.

It is in these times that I release the tensions that kept me bound to who I thought I was. I am no longer shackled to my yesterdays or even a wish of tomorrow. I am at peace and able to travel in the timeless universe within ourself.

A moment before, there were a thousand things that were missing or needing to be done. Now nothing is missing and nothing needs to be done.

When I am in these moments, I feel a compassion for the me, who a moment ago seemed lost, shouting into the face of the wild wind of life.

And I feel a sadness that he should feel so burdened and unnecessarily alone. I see that we two, the lost of me and the found of me, are family, we are both me. We are inseparable on this earth, and no amount of contempt or self-blame can ever break this truth. It is what makes us human. It is what has made the songs of humanity's journey on earth throughout the ages.

Without the dark, the light would not know who it was.
Without the light, we can never create the stars to guide us from the shadow of ourselves.

*I know enough to know what I feel is real and
know enough to know not its whole truth.*

*What if this divine aspect, is more than just a
children's bedtime story? What if it is a fraction of
God within, with all the power of creation by its side?
And what if the spirit within each human has the
power to touch the universe, to see the lights that
guide our way, to hear the songs that bring to life the
flowers, the oceans, and the air that we breathe?*

How can the mind perceive of this, cope with the
enormity of this power and its richness?

If we were not a part of Creation then it would be
impossible. But it is not a foreign land, but it is
bewildering to those parts of us that see nothing but
a finite world and a finite life.

It's understandable. There is just too much that is
willing to dismiss such thoughts of grandeur, too
much urging me to keep within the limits of what is
known. To play the game that what we know is all
that is. The trouble is, that way of living makes us
feel unseen, alone, and fragile, yet within the greater
vision of life, we are neither unseen, alone or fragile.

It is a paradox that these two lives that seem so
different, so apparently at odds, are actually one life,
my life. That this great illumined, loving being that I
can find within myself, is part of me, as is the me
that struggles to see the light within a day.

So, can I love the pained me as I love the beautiful me? I'm not sure that creation sees a difference; for within the dark, we do create paths of light, and in the fire of our struggle, forge courage, hope, dedication, and love; precious gems, lights that are revered by the creators of life.

There is a purpose and a life that exists beyond belief, outside of the lamentations of what I see as true, beyond the wall of the assumptions I have about the possibility of life. So, I will do my sacred work of remembering to remember the divine within and loving the me that journeys there.

What words will surrender this greater dream to earthly existence. What inherent ability will honour the unique purpose of my creation?

Without me, God cannot see.

When I bring my consciousness back from its wanderings and become present to myself, without judgment of what is. It is then that I become a soul purpose again, conscious of myself and creation. I become an act and a witness of creation and creation sees itself through me.

Without God, I cannot hear.

Without the presence in me of that universal something, my perception becomes scattered to the winds of time. I become lost to the truth of who I really am and can no longer hear the subtle sound of the moment's meaning.

But when I am touching this divine within myself, the orchestra lights up and the air fills with the meanings of life, its colours and its song.

Without people, I cannot speak.

Without the lives of others, there is no flow, no giving and receiving of life. There is no conversation, no intimate sharing of the loves of life.

There would never be the thousand million moments of love's endeavour on earth. For when two or more creators share their creations, share their loves of life, more than what was shared happens. It calls in the cause of creation, the presence of love.

When I can do this, I honour the purpose of my humanity on earth.

THE GREATEST GIFT OF GOD IS ITS ABSENCE?

To be God-like without the knowledge of God is no mean feat.

To create moments of love day after day without the known comfort of the love of creation, is a profound thing. But then to muster the courage to share these loves with another is a sublime act of trust.

That is love.

To gather a singular consciousness of self from the witness and experience of life. And then to be given the free will to choose what to be and how to be it, is impressive enough. But we are also given the profound ability to choose the self-defining act of 'why' we do it.

All this without the sense of the infinite nature of life. That is God-like in its inspiration.

To build a world within the mind, to create a truth of the truth, with thought, feeling and reason, and then to rebuild it every day.

All this without knowing the benign nature of life. That is fortitude.

To create a picture of what tomorrow may be, to bring it close with intention and then mould it with purpose and love.

All this without the awareness of the indigenous flow of life. That is hope.

To honour the value of your life with acts and accomplishments. And then to share this in kinship to another person.

All this without the known company of the universe. That is courage.

To make a home and family with love and to give space and peace so others may grow. To give paternal light, warmth, comfort, and joy without the known kinship of creation.

That is grace.

All these are not casual gifts, they are Godlike abilities that nurture and create life. They are sparks of humanity that augment the fabric of humanities consciousness.

They are testaments to the divine nature of being human, to being made in the image of God.

I believe we carry a hunger for a possibility of life. A vision that exists at the edge of our perception and in the depths of our heart. It is a time when we walk in love and where the loves we create of life never fade. A time when we live the inspiration of who we are and where the turbulent waters of the heart are forever stilled. It is a dream of love. And our acts of life are our attempts to bring this dream to earth.

This story of love has been carried over time by millions of people for thousands of years. People who, through their acts of kindness, inspiration and courage, have conceived and created humanity's journey on earth. Now we, at the leading edge of love's timeline, are its custodians and its hope.

The final story of the work has been inspired from humanity's struggle to breathe life into this vision and the mythologies written about it in ancient times.

Once upon a time, before time had been created, we did not know a tomorrow or a yesterday. We lived as children within the maternal realm of mother earth. She fed and nurtured us as we grew to know the wonders of life. We did not know pain or strife for all was under the kind eye of the paternal father who gave permission of what could and could not be.

We lived within an atmosphere where all was known and our thoughts and feelings were guided by parental love. It was a place where all that we thought came about and all that came about was held in place. We did not forget what we loved for it was what we lived.

191

It was easy as there was no distance between the power of cause and its earthly creation.

This was a heaven on earth. But the time was soon approaching when we would come of age, would leave the nest of given ease. We would create our own meaning of life and become conscious.

This would not be easy for the light that gave us life would no longer be visible. It would seem as if a great darkness had befallen us, that we were alone and without kinship.

Of course, this would not be true, but we would nevertheless face a dire journey without the comfort of a known path.

But it had to be, for we had become restless in a world of everything. We sought a different world, a place where we could learn another meaning of ourselves.

So, it was granted, and the grace and power that had been given to nurture our young lives was slowly withdrawn. What was, would become but a memory, and its truth would settle into the deep heart of ourselves.

Over time this would become hidden by the calamity of life, its truth but a forgotten dream. For now, we entered a strange and foreboding place. It would seem as if we had been forsaken, abandoned to an endless winter, bereft of light and warmth. We were no longer in love, we had to create it.

So, we did, day after day we struggled to bring the light and the warmth. But no sooner had we created it, it would then dissolve, be washed away by the torrent of life of this new world. So, in the cold light of each morning, we would begin again.

This temporary nature of things was new to us, for in the world before time, what we created never left us; it was an endless act of love. But now our feelings of life were no longer stable, they changed from moment to moment.

It was as if we were born again and had to learn to breathe, to decide for ourselves what should and should not be. And we did, we made millions of decisions over thousands of years and created a thousand paths from our hearts, dewdrops of life squeezed out between the powers of light and dark.

As time grew old it began to loosen its grip on the mind of man. The veil of separation started to lift and our sense of life began to change. We felt the edges of the finite world and sensed a world beyond what we thought was real.

This was not an easy time, for although we longed to be reunited with the heaven held in our heart, we had become accustomed to the craggy world of our disbelief. It was at least known, and because of that, secure. But it was too late to go back, it was after all our choice to remake ourselves. And we now stood at the dawn of that achievement. We had done enough to allow its call to pull us forward and we had done enough to know of our irrevocable arrival.

Why the feather?

When I was a teenager, I was struck by the ancient Egyptian story of the heart being measured against the feather of truth. This seemed such a powerful yet impossible thing to be done. How could the heart, that it was believed carried the residue of our feelings of life, be as light as a feather? But the thought that it could be inspires me to this day. Now, whenever I see or pick up a feather, I am reminded of the feelings I can muster, acts I can do that will lighten the heart of me.

I do know that when my heart is light, I see more clearly and love more dearly.

Whatever is the heart of you carries your own words, not mine.

The final exercises are to sum up the feelings you have gathered from this journey.

Exercise 1: *Write the key points that you have discovered from yourself within this journey. Understandings that gave you a sense of freedom and love that you want to remember.*

_____

_____

_____

_____

_____

_____

_____

_____

_____

_____

_____

_____

_____

_____

_____

Exercise 2: A daily remembrance of what is important for you is always wise. What image or words can you write each day that can help you remember what it is that you love?

THE FINAL WORD

During the last year of writing this book, a word kept impressing itself upon me, as if it's a missing key that I have lost or yet to truly find. I have given it mention a few times in this work, but have yet to really define a meaning.

Perhaps because it is such a tricky word. it has obvious meaning in the outer world of things, but in the inner world of ourselves it is not so straight forward.

The word appears to my mind whenever I drill down into the core of me, or when I search for the next invisible step, and always if I touch the divine nature of things. It is a word that denotes our deepest choice of what we will be and what we will allow. It is what we are open to, without conditions or expectations.

The word is Trust.

It is a quality that is easy for an innocent child to live. But for an adult, it can be the greatest of challenges. To trust is to let go of ourselves and take a leap of faith. But faith needs to have a good reason, some substance as to why we should trust. It has to be earned. We will trust another person when they have given us the belief that they intend us no harm. But to trust the intangibility of our heart or to trust creation is not so easy, it makes us exposed and vulnerable.

No one can tell another what to trust. They may show us why, may even be a living embodiment of a trust we want to have. But we will always have to make it ours; decide for ourself, where in life we will step with the vision of trust.

Trust is the destiny builder, the ultimate choice of what we will give ourselves to. It is what we are willing to surrender our conscious self to, because trust is always a step into the unknown.

We cannot know ourself fully. We are such a diverse universe of life. And life itself is just too big, way too big to be held in the conscious mind. But when we take courage and trust life and trust ourselves, we surrender our own world for something greater. When we do trust the rewards are immeasurable. We become part of the greater world and that great world becomes part of us.

When I trust the heart of me, it gives me faith in who I am. It sets my mind free from the exhausting second guessing of each moment. I become in company with my dearest fried and I fall in love with life easily. It is a trust that allows a communion with the core of me, and if I am patient in that journey, the divine of me.

It is my greatest hope that this book has given you inspiration to trust your heart. To think of it as a wise companion. A part of you that cares for your well-being and holds the key to the greatest you.

We have come to the end of this journey to the heart for now. Thank you for joining me in its story of adventure. I hope the experience empowered you as much as it did me. And that your willingness to embrace the vulnerable heart of yourself has been enriched. You will not be disappointed at what you will find there.

NOTES ON THE JOURNEY

(To cut out and keep)

1. *Ultimately it is lack of self-love that always eroded our communion to the heart.*

2. *Our consciousness can only be conscious according to the remit that our feelings give it.*

3. *The actual moments of life will always be more than our memories can give it.*

4. *Our beliefs are our law of attraction, and like a magnet, they will power our minds attention and intention.*

5. *We may always choose the reason for what we do, decide its purpose, and create its meaning. This 'why' is the ultimate tool of our self-definition.*

6. *Our will is equal to the power we have in the why-we-do-what-we-do. It is through our will that we maintain our integrity and with that, our authenticity.*

7. *The freedom we seek is nurtured in the mystery of life and in the acceptance of the mystery of ourselves.*

8. *The heart is the source of our truth, not the truth of yesterday or tomorrow that the mind struggles to know, but the truth of the moment, the living truth.*

9. Knowing the heart - *What paths can we make, what signs have we created to see the journey home, to re-join the conversation with our beloved self?*

10. Being Human - *If we do not embrace the human part of ourselves, we will always be dismayed at its appearance.*

11. *You cannot love in fear and you do not fear in love.*

12. Vulnerability and fragility - *To be open and vulnerable to ourselves is not always comfortable, but it is always our truth.*

13. Learning to love yourself - *Learning to love yourself is tricky because you have to be soft to the parts of yourself that make you hard.*

14. Love - *Be not timid with your love for no great life ever happened without it*

15. Forgiveness - *We always do our best but sometimes do not forgive ourselves for not being perfect.*

16. *Diving the divine...only your words belong here.*